Every Day

40 Strategies to Deepen Learning in Any Class

Dr. Nathan D. Lang-Raad

WeVideo Every Day

© 2019 by Nathan D. Lang-Raad, EdD

These books are available at special discounts when purchased in quantity for use as premiums, promotions, fundraising and educational use. For inquiries and details, contact the publisher: edtechteam.com/press.

Published by EdTechTeam Press

Library of Congress Control Number: On File

Paperback ISBN: 978-1-945167-57-7
eBook ISBN: 978-1-945167-58-4

Irvine, California

CONTENTS

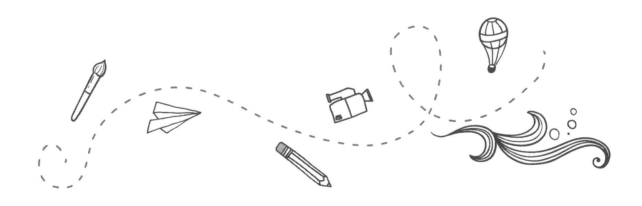

INTRODUCTION

Used by millions of students in every grade and subject area, WeVideo empowers learners to discover their voice and make an impact in their world. WeVideo's platform promotes deeper learning while making it fun and easy for students to express their ideas with creativity and authenticity.

The most successful learning occurs when teachers are facilitators or activators of learning. Instead of giving formulaic sets of worksheets, tasks, or practice problems, teachers today are designing active, engaging learning experiences that build on student strengths and interests. During these learning experiences, students are empowered to think in more complex ways while creating and engaging with content through real-life problem-solving and perseverance.

WeVideo has created a platform that supports student-centered learning so you can:

- Create an environment where students feel safe and empowered.
- Clearly communicate goals in a fun and engaging way.
- See learning in action.
- Provide a structure for students to share their voice with their peers, the community, and the world.
- Engage students at deeper learning through critical thinking and creativity.

This book offers forty strategies that empower you and your students to use WeVideo to deepen learning and spawn creativity. Try out the ideas, and share your students' creations online using the hashtag #wevideoeveryday!

EASY BEGINNING PROJECT

Anyone can create videos! Everyone should create videos! Introduce yourself in thirty seconds.

Grade Levels:	Time:	Learning Goals:	Support:
K–12	30 minutes	Students will learn the foundations of how to create a video in WeVideo.	Allow students to explore and have fun. Provide directions in a Google Doc to help students guide their own experiences. Circulate around the classroom to support and affirm students.

INSTRUCTIONS

1. Go to wevideo.com.
2. Click *Log In* in the top right corner.
3. Click the red *Log In with Google* button.
4. You may need to click on your name.
5. If a black screen comes up, press the *Refresh* key.
6. Click the black *Create New* button option on the screen. (If this is not your first WeVideo project, the button will be blue.)
7. To make sure you're working in Timeline Mode, click on the three lines in the top left corner. Scroll down and click on the *Timeline Mode* choice if it is showing. (If it is not visible, you are already in Timeline Mode!)
8. Add a title section by clicking on the text button—it has a letter *A* on it. Choose a layout and drag it into the beginning of video 1. Double-click the text slide from within your timeline to edit the text.

9. Click the "Media" button (file folder with a star on it) to upload some images. Click the green upload arrow to import the images.
10. Click the blue *Browse to Select* button and browse to your images. Alternatively, click on *My Drive* on the left side of the menu at the bottom of the box.
11. Search for three image files that you want to download. If you'd like, you can search for any images directly inside the Star Video library. Some ideas for images you could use include a picture of your favorite spot in the school, you making a goofy face, favorite animal, etc.
12. Click on the images so they all turn blue. Hold down the Control key while selecting to choose more than one image.
13. Click the blue *Open* button (computer) or *Select* button (Drive).
14. Wait for the images to upload.
15. Drag the three images onto the *Video 1* line.

16. You can also capture your own video by clicking the red button:

> You will be presented with two options: create a webcam recording or a screen recording. Select either *Record Screen* or *Webcam* and click *Continue*.

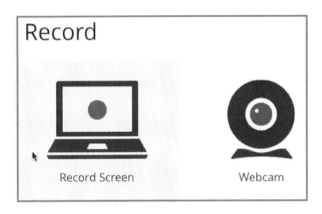

17. When finished, scroll up and click *Finish Video* at the top.
18. Provide a title by typing your name and an animal; for example, Andy Animal.
19. Click the blue *Set* button.
20. Select the *720 HD* choice and then click the Drive icon so they both turn blue.
21. Click the blue *Finish Video* button. Watch it load!
22. Once it is finished loading, download and share it to YouTube.

Tips & Extensions

WeVideo regularly updates and enhances the app and platform experience so that your students can create like never before.

Please visit the links below for the most updated tutorials on navigating the platform:

- wevideo.com/education
- wevideo.com/academy

GREEN SCREEN PROJECT

Change the entire feel of a video, convey a strong message, or create special effects using green screen technology.

Grade Levels:	Time:	Learning Goals:	Support:
K–5	45 minutes	Students will build creativity and problem-solving skills by using the green screen feature.	A few steps are needed in this process to ensure a "clean" green screen. Teachers should consider chunking the steps and providing checkpoints along the way before moving on to the subsequent steps.

INSTRUCTIONS

1. **Green Screen:** Also known as chroma key or color keying, green screen is a special effect/post-production technique used to composite two clips together. This technique allows you to remove a single color from your video—usually the background of a video recorded in front of an evenly lit green or blue screen (like the weather forecaster at your local news station). These are preferable choices because skin pigments don't naturally have these colors.

2. **Color Keying Basics:** To create the effect, you'll need a minimum of two clips and two layers in the Timeline Editing Mode. One clip will serve as your background (e.g., a beach image), and the other is a video clip that should be recorded in front of an evenly lit solid background (generally green or blue).

3. **Creating the Effect:**

   ### Step 1: Lay the pieces

   Drop the background on the main track then drag the "green screen" video in the track on top of the background.

   ### Step 2: Remove the color

   To open the Color Keying controls, double-click on the green screen video and switch to the Color Keying tab (looks like a person's head and shoulders). Select the color that you want to remove (also known as the key color) with the help of the dropper tool. Try to get a sample in an area that is evenly lit while avoiding other colors. If you get too close to other colors, you might pick up more than one and the effect won't look as smooth.

Step 3: Defining the mask

WeVideo automatically removes the color and creates a mask that defines areas in your video that are transparent and opaque. To see the mask, locate the *Mask* option and select it.

The mask is a black-and-white representation of the image. The black areas represent transparent sections of your video that will be replaced with your background image. White areas represent opaque ones that will maintain the original video (your subject).

The goal when color keying is to refine the mask so the color in question can be removed as much as possible. Use the sliders to edit the mask, and constantly switch between *Image* and *Mask* to understand how the different controls affect the mask.

Once students have mastered the green screen tool, they can incorporate this effect for any of the lessons and projects in this book.

Tips & Extensions

Work with the sliders until the students get a good mask. This will require some trial and error, so be patient!

Make sure you check your mask at different moments of your video to ensure it looks good throughout the video. If you need to tweak it in only one section, split the clip by pressing S on your keyboard and then correct the new clip.

NEED GREEN SCREEN HELP?

Jennifer Leban, a creative technology teacher in Elmhurst, Illinois, is a pro at green screen projects. For more info on how WeVideo "green screen" works, check out her video: youtu.be/dncfSreR25E

For more green screen ideas, check out her videos here: youtu.be/cWdqSEzlNXc

lebanteachtech.com

3 SCREENCASTING

Screencasting is a great tool both to visually represent thinking and to showcase or explain something.

Grade Levels:	**Learning Goals:**	**Support:**
K–5	Students will be able to create a video to showcase the steps involved in researching, informational writing, and speaking skills.	As with any presentation, students should prepare with notes, storyboards, or a mockup. With early grades, students can prepare with pictures. Encourage students and reaffirm them if they make mistakes. Remind them they can always stop the video recording to organize their materials or collect their thoughts, then start again.
Time: 30 minutes		

INSTRUCTIONS

Screen Recording enables your students to record a video of their entire computer screen or a single desktop window. Any actions that you take on the screen, such as scrolling or clicking, will be recorded. Once you finish recording, you can save the recording as a video and use it within WeVideo.

Please note that screen recording is only available on premium accounts and requires the latest Google Chrome browser update.

1. To begin, click on the *Record* button in your media gallery.

2. You will be presented with two options to create: a webcam recording or a screen recording.

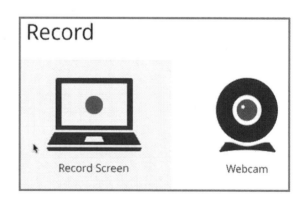

3. Select *Record Screen* and click *Continue*.

4. You have the option to record the entire screen or just a specific open window. You also have the option to record a voiceover while screen recording. Click *Continue* after making your choices.

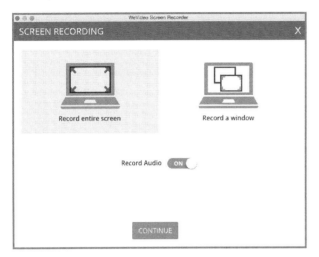

5. Select your screen or window and click *Share* to begin.

6. You will know that it is recording when you see this status

7. When you are finished recording, click *Stop sharing*. You will then be able to preview what you just recorded

8. You can start over by clicking *Record New*. If you are happy with your recording, you can click *Download* to save a video file of your recording locally or you can click *Save* to immediately upload it to WeVideo.

9. When the upload has completed, you can use your screen recording just like any other video file.

Tips & Extensions

Screencasting would be a great tool for any of the following:

- Routines and procedures
- Giving student feedback
- Recording lessons to upload to Google Classroom or another LMS for student interaction
- Digital storytelling
- Student reflections on learning
- Flipped lessons

4 BOOK TALKS

Engage students in reading by having them present a book in a fun, persuasive, and suspenseful commercial.

Grade Levels:	**Learning Goals:**	**Support:**
K–12	Students will build communication, presentation, and listening skills while creating a commercial for a book.	Create an exemplar book talk video for your students to demonstrate what a book talk video might look like. When recording, engage your viewers in the book talk as if you were talking to students live. Ask them questions (these can be titles on your screen) and have them guess what will happen next.
Time: 30 minutes		

INSTRUCTIONS

1. Create a one- to five-minute video of this "book commercial" for students. First, choose a book you want to create the book talk around. The book can be centered around a theme (e.g., Black History Month, Women's History Month, LGBT Pride Month), or choose a book written in first person with characters that reflect the students' experiences.

2. Once you choose the book, think about the elements (e.g., resonating quotes, cliffhangers) you want to include in the book talk video. Record your thoughts and reflections in a Google Doc or sticky notes placed in the book.

3. Begin the book talk with a hook. The hook could be a reenactment of your favorite scene or a suspenseful part in the book. Think about a movie trailer and the elements that make it exciting and build suspense. Although you might be tempted to begin with the cover and author, save that for the end! You want to keep the students wondering about the book.

4. Continue the book talk by telling a story, referencing quotes, or playing one of the characters in the story (i.e., dress up, take on an accent)! Leave your students wanting to know more by creating a cliffhanger at the end. You want your students to have more questions and to be enthusiastic about reading the book you chose! Ask students to respond to your book talk before they begin reading the book.

5. Ask students to create their own book talk with a book of their choice. Provide a note-taking template or guide to help them summarize the story. The questions below can help guide students through making their own book talk:

Book Talk Guide

- What is the hook (e.g., attention grabber, suspense generator)?
- What were your favorite quotes?
- What are some specific details to support your opinion of the book?
- Who were your favorite characters?
- What is a strong reason for the audience to read the book?
- Did you save the cover and author for the end?
- What is the cliffhanger at the end?

Tips & Extensions

Let your students choose a book that has a motivating theme that will be of interest to your entire class. In elementary school, books about family, animals, toys, and nature will resonate. In middle and high school, books about love, humor, magic, science fiction, friendship, and relationships will be a big hit.

A SCHOOL TESTIMONIAL

I also go online and watch YouTubers talk about how to have better lighting and better sound. I work with my staff and we laugh all the time on what we could add to our videos. We try to go over the top with everything we do. We don't just want to talk about the book; we want a dragon or alligator trying to eat us, or later spitting out a teacher. Remember, that's the hook. That's what they'll remember. If you show them a dragon, or if you shrink yourself into a book, that's what they'll go home and talk about and why they'll watch it ten more times. So if you don't have a hook, you don't get their attention.

—Andy Jacks, *elementary school principal, Ashland, Virginia*

5 ANIMAL RESEARCH PROJECT

Inspired by Jennifer Eggert, instructional technology coach, Bloomingdale, Illinois

Instead of creating a written report about an animal, try this engaging and interactive approach!

Grade Levels:	Time:	Learning Goals:	Support:
K–5	Three instructional days	Students will be able to create a video to showcase the steps of researching, informational writing, and speaking skills.	Even with the trend of increasing video projects, whether expository or informative, practicing writing remains essential for students. This video project can be done in conjunction with a writing component, allowing the writing piece to be more interactive and spark creativity.

INSTRUCTIONS

1. Students choose a rainforest animal based on classroom texts.
2. Students will begin by researching animals. This search can be done right in the WeVideo platform. Search for snakes, and licensed videos and still images of snakes will appear.
3. Record the reading of the informational paragraph aloud in front of the green screen, using the WeVideo webcam.

   - Allow students to bring in props.
   - Project words on a projector screen or hold paper close by for students to read.

4. Use the WeVideo editor to enhance the video research:

   - Green screen layering
   - Add a title
   - Upload videos as background
   - Scale the image
   - Increase the volume
   - Publish the video

- Create a playlist in YouTube so students can access one another's videos. Ask students to reflect on their own video and those of their classmates.
- Self-reflect by filling out a rubric or checklist and answering questions
- Give peer feedback
- Make a plan for their next research video

Tips & Extensions

- Install Text-to-Speech extensions so websites can be read to students.
- Practice fluency by reading paragraphs aloud.
- While students are in reflection, ask them to make a plan for their next video research project.

EXIT TICKET

Exit tickets provide quick, effective checks for understanding and formative assessment. Exit tickets are no longer confined to small slips of paper collected by teachers as students leave their classrooms. Video exit tickets allow for teachers to see body language and facial expressions and assess students' communication skills.

Grade Levels:
K–12

Time:
10 minutes

Learning Goals:
Students will track progress toward learning goals by reflection via a video exit ticket.

Support:
Before students create their video exit ticket, teachers should model a video reflection for them. Ask students to notice specific reflective practices, such as questions that still exist, how thinking is expressed, academic vocabulary, and specific evidence of learning referenced.

INSTRUCTIONS

1. After a lesson or classroom task, allow students to reflect on their learning through a video exit ticket.
2. Allow students to whisper practice their recording or jot down their reflection before they create their videos.
3. Provide question stems for students as they create their exit ticket videos.

Examples of question stems:
- How did I conclude?
- Why did I think this is the case?
- What is the most important thing I learned?
- What was my favorite part?
- What was my least favorite part?

Tips & Extensions

Allow students to find a space to record their video reflection. This can be done at their desk or at your video creation makerspace. If students need alone time, allow them to record at home or find a supervised place at school where they can spread out.

Teachers can encourage students to talk on video about arguments that are focused on both how and why they did what they did or about what they believe. The classroom culture must support curiosity and sense making, which is reflected in terms of both the questions that students pose to one another and the questions that students address in their reflection videos.

MORNING NEWS SHOW

Inspired by Jennifer Eggert, instructional coach, Bloomingdale, Illinois

Start the learning day off on the best foot by replacing intercom announcements with a morning news show.

Grade Levels:
K–12

Time:
30 minutes

Learning Goals:
Students will create videos to build communication and speaking skills.

Support:
Creating a script template might be helpful so students can fill in their own outlines. Add subtitles for English-language learners (ELL), and add audio text recordings to accompany plain text for younger students.

INSTRUCTIONS

Ask newscaster students to draft an outline of topics they'd like to include; after you review and give feedback on student outlines, they are ready to create their videos. Can they write the script? Can they generate the ideas? Is it possible for students to help with the filming? What about students editing the video? These are questions that can help guide the level of support and how much time you want to provide students in the creation of the news show.

You can help spawn creative ideas by providing some options:

- Welcome
- The Pledge of Allegiance
- Daily/weekly announcements
- Student work spotlight
- Thought of the day
- Weather
- This day in history
- Looking ahead
- Root word raps
- Math projects around school
- Science experiments
- Riddles
- Book talks
- Famous quotes
- Ellen DeGeneres's "Game of Games"
- Culture/holiday spotlight
- Vocabulary words of the day
- Content area trivia
- Dance battles
- Teacher interviews
- Workout/exercise/yoga
- Magic tricks
- Random acts of kindness challenges

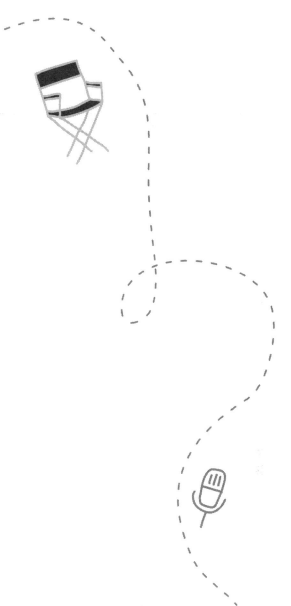

Tips & Extensions

- Make the announcements as student-led as possible.

- The WeVideo platform includes a built-in "Newscast" template.

- Keep features short and simple!

- Visuals are key. Keep 'em coming!

- Challenge middle and high school students to change the script structure each week.

Use the morning announcements as an opportunity to create school pride. This is also an opportunity to learn about what makes an effective video production set. Building a production area is key. Here are a few helpful set items:

- Well-lit room

- Camera for recording

- Devices for editing

- Props

- Fake or real microphones

- Green screen

- Timer

- Teleprompter app

CONCRETE LEARNING GOALS

A vivid picture of the future makes it seem more real and thus easier to prioritize. Learning goals are pictures of the future; they should be communicated with concrete visuals so students feel motivated to meet them.

Grade Levels:	Learning Goals:	Support:
K–5	Students will be able to clearly articulate learning goals.	A student-friendly math goal might look like this: "I can use multiplication within 100 to solve word problems in situations involving equal groups, arrays, and measurement quantities." In this scenario, the teacher plans on using a 100-box grid and two dice. To make the game and strategy clear, the teacher should create a video that showcases the items used in the game.
Time: 15 minutes		

INSTRUCTIONS

1. The key for this instructional strategy is to create a student-friendly learning goal with concrete language.
2. Next, decide what imagery and props you want to include in the video. Be creative with your learning goal video.
3. Dress up as a fictional character or mathematical savant.
4. Clearly articulate the learning goal and use titles to reinforce the learning goal.

Tips & Extensions

Visual representations are effective learning strategies, but this isn't always meaningful for students unless they see an example right from the beginning of the lesson. The visuals should be presented throughout the lesson, until the students have built understanding.

Ask students to create their own videos to show evidence that they not only understand the learning goal but have mastered it.

GUIDED RECIPROCAL PEER QUESTIONING

Use this formative strategy to practice questioning and reflection.

Grade Levels:
3–12

Time:
30 minutes

Learning Goals:
Students will be able to create a video of their guided reciprocal peer questioning. The process will help students build inquiry skills while constructing questions. At the same time, students also develop metacognition skills through reflection.

Support:
Guided reciprocal peer questioning is an example of a formative assessment. This exercise should not only provide teachers with quick and ongoing checks for understanding but also should provide students with opportunities to learn while being assessed. The process described here ensures that both assessment and learning occur simultaneously.

INSTRUCTIONS

1. Teachers can provide scaffolding for this strategy by first issuing multiple question prompts for students to choose from and then eventually asking students to create their own prompts. To aid in question generation, it's useful to refer to the learning protocol of building probing questions. Former economist and educator Charlotte Danielson developed a framework for teaching that includes five questions that teachers can use for guided reciprocal peer questioning:

- Why do you think this is the case?
- What would you have to change in order for . . . ?
- What do you assume to be true about . . . ?
- How did you conclude . . . ?
- How did your assumptions influence how you thought about . . . ?

2. For guided reciprocal peer questioning, teachers provide prompts during small group collaborative learning and the appropriate amount of time (ten to fifteen minutes) to conduct the learning experience.

3. Students open WeVideo and record themselves discussing the prompts. As students discuss the prompts, the teacher circulates and records observations and supports the video creation process.

Tips & Extensions

The key component of this strategy is capturing student reflection and thinking. Students should plan for what they will ask before capturing video. Will they take turns, follow a certain order, show any visuals, etc.? Planning could happen on note cards or in Google Docs.

10 DIGITAL PORTFOLIOS

Learning portfolios, traditionally made up of binders of student work or loose student work hung on a bulletin board, have taken a new shape in the digital age. Digital learning portfolios provide students with innovative ways to self-document and showcase their learning through the creation of videos.

Grade Levels:
K–12

Time:
30 minutes

Learning Goals:
Students will be able to create a video to showcase the process of conducting research, informational writing, and speaking skills.

Support:
Learning portfolios also can serve as a final product during an inquiry-based or project-based learning experience. Because this assessment strategy more closely emulates real-world work, students are highly motivated and become true curators of their own learning while also providing the teacher with data to use for appropriate feedback on current levels of learning. It's important for teachers to provide guidance on what should be included in the portfolio.

INSTRUCTIONS

1. Learning portfolios not only provide an effective means of authentic assessment for teachers but they also give parents and other students a window into rigorous and relevant learning. The following ideas show an example of the contents of a learning portfolio for any grade level:

   - Daily learning reflections
   - Exit tickets
   - A challenging problem showing good reasoning and problem-solving skills
   - Proof of how the student went from confusion to understanding
   - Student preference for their best-fit strategy with explanation
   - Activity and task reflections and corrections
   - Proof of collaboration, with justification for why it is good
   - Think-alouds
   - Unit projects
   - Something the student is really proud of (with explanation)
   - Collection of visual representations used to solve problems or articulate ideas
   - Collection of student-created explainer videos

Tips & Extensions

It's important to ensure that students specifically align the content of learning portfolios to learning objectives and goals. The representation of student work or products is linked to the reflective component of the learning portfolio, and it is driven by purpose (real-world application of concepts) and audience (an authentic audience in addition to the teacher).

2. The last section of the portfolio can be used as a comprehensive reflection. The following questions serve as reflection prompts:

- What is something you are most proud of?
- What was the hardest concept you encountered this year, and how did you conquer it? What is the evidence of your progression?
- What is something you would do differently next time?
- Choose a performance task that you're most proud of and talk about the practices you used to create a solution.
- Looking over your work from the beginning of the learning portfolio to the end, what evidence shows growth in either your processes or your concept understanding?
- How will you use your learning portfolio going forward? Did you find the process valuable?

11 PODCASTS

Contributed by Jeffrey Bradbury, technology integration specialist and creator of the TeacherCast Educational Network

Podcasting allows students' voices to be heard and gives them a platform to communicate their experiences and thinking.

Grade Levels: 3-8 **Time:** 1 hour	**Learning Goals:** Students will collaborate and create their own podcast with a topic of their choice.	**Support:** The process of podcasting involves outlining, creating a narrative, and selecting major themes. Students will need support on identifying the main idea, collecting supporting details, revising, and editing.

INSTRUCTIONS

1. Each student group begins by researching their idea or concept (depending on the context of your classroom). Google Docs can be used to compose a general outline for how the podcast will be set up.

2. Students use iPhones and iPads to interview teachers on their recollection of the students' chosen project topics. To prepare for this, talk about interviewing skills in class and conduct mock interviews within student groups to sound as professional as possible.

3. To divide and conquer this project as quickly as possible, encourage the groups to split up the work. Students in each group should be assigned jobs ranging from "researcher" to "music selector," "audio engineer," and "interviewer." This experience reinforces collaboration and teamwork.

4. Finally, put the projects together and create the podcast. Students may upload all of their audio clips into a shared Google Drive folder. This allows them to collectively and collaboratively build their sequenced podcast into the WeVideo platform.

Tips & Extensions

- Exciting new update for WeVideo, an audio only export: bit.ly/2PiHiCQ

- For more on recording a voiceover, check out this tutorial: bit.ly/WVvoiceover

- This video provides a tutorial on how to use WeVideo as a podcasting platform: bit.ly/WVGetStarted

- Encourage students to create an outline instead of a script. A podcast should be more conversational and not rehearsed.

- HyperDocs are Google Docs that take the student through a process step by step with the inclusion of links to resources. They are a great way to help students organize their podcasts. A good example of a HyperDoc guiding the user through a podcast creation project by Jennifer Wolfe is found here: bit.ly/2vfGDcc

- Students should record in pairs. One student should act as an interviewer and the other as an interviewee.

- Provide a platform for students to listen to other students' podcasts. This could be done simply through a Google Drive folder.

—*Contributor: Jennifer Wolfe, middle school teacher, Davis, California*

12 LENDING PROJECT WITH KIVA

This project can provide experiences through which students gain knowledge and skills by working for an extended period to investigate and respond to an authentic, engaging, and complex question, problem, or challenge.

Grade Levels:
5-8

Time:
Five instructional days

Learning Goals:
Students will use operations with decimals to solve a real-world problem and explain their reasoning through models. Additionally, students can present an opinion by sequencing ideas logically and using appropriate facts and relevant descriptive details to support their main ideas.

Support:
Video creation adapts readily to project-based learning across grade levels, subject areas, and differentiated student needs.

INSTRUCTIONS

1. Provide students with the following scenario:

   - In the role of financial advisor, you are challenged to find the best way to impact a community with only $25. You will select a project from the organization Kiva.org to provide a $25 microloan. This website connects the lender to the borrower.

   - Fellow students, teachers, and community members will be the investors. To help you determine the best use of the funds, you will conduct interviews with a banker to learn how lending works and with investors to learn about which projects they are most passionate about. You should be thinking about the potential impact of your chosen project on the surrounding community, not just for the borrower.

   - You will factor in repayment schedules, as well as delinquency and default rates, for the given project and borrower. You will be in charge of taking the funds and investing them into Kiva.org so the borrowers can begin their projects.

   - The end product will be a student-created video that will be shared with all the investors, as well as the school and the local community, with the goal of getting your Kiva project fully funded.

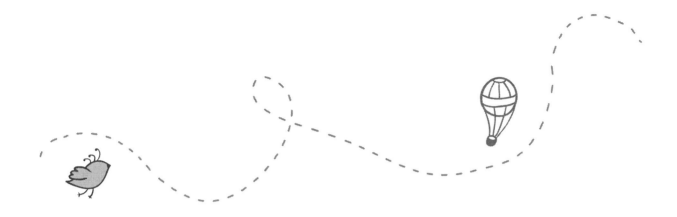

2. Students first collaboratively develop a plan for their video by creating a storyboard. The video should include media (e.g., photos, music, graphics) and interview clips from the borrower's community. Students will have a choice as to whom they interview and will determine how to sequence the story to generate the most impact. If students are unable to interview the borrower they can use the information provided on the site. Each loan includes a description of the borrower, usually translated from their own words, so this part could feature one of the students reading an excerpt of that description and explaining how that description influenced them to choose that particular loan for their project.

3. The video should include the students' own thoughts and opinions predicting the future success of the borrower. It will also explain why they believe this project will make the biggest impact on that borrower's community.

Tips & Extensions

Project-based learning principles provide a canvas on which students collect research and drive insights. They are empowered to reveal novel insights they make by establishing connections across rich material. Such projects provide teachers with formative assessment opportunities to simultaneously appraise how students perceive the project and to evaluate their skill levels across multiple areas.

Source: Adapted from BIE.org, which holds it as a "Gold Standard" example of a project. The original was developed by National Faculty members Angela Marzilli and Erika Jordan.

13 CREATIVE EXPEDITIONS

Turn creativity into practical educational experiences and meaningful projects. It's not enough to only provide direction. Students need a tool to help them get there.

Grade Levels:
3–12

Time:
Varies depending on the scope of the expedition

Learning Goals:
Students will amplify their voices and make their own decisions about how they will go on an expedition.

Support:
When engaged in video creation, students may struggle with the multitude of options available to them, including the sequence of their video story, the variety of media available to incorporate, and identifying concepts that are most effective for sharing their stories.

INSTRUCTIONS

Teachers can use the questions, prompts, and inspiration below to help their students more effectively design, plan, and storyboard options as they engage in video creation projects. The creative expeditions can be used for any projects, from book reviews to historical documentaries.

The 4Cs for Creative Expeditions

1. Why do I **care**? Why would others care?

   Imagine the finished video project in your mind or draw it out. Does it elicit emotion? Is it meaningful to you personally? Is it exciting?

   GUIDING QUESTION: Why must I create this video? What problem am I solving?

What do I ultimately want to express?

INSPIRATION: Watch these first graders get excited about viewing *Reading Rainbow* book reviews. Students can design the process for making their own (bit.ly/2YKw3aV).

2. What are my **criteria**?

   Identify the criteria that you will use to align, measure, and critically assess your video creation project.

   GUIDING QUESTION: How will I know when I'm successful?

   INSPIRATION: Read how one teacher teaches the nine elements of digital

Tips & Extensions

Few things are as daunting as a blank page or an empty timeline. This strategy is best used before engaging in a project, but it also could be used as a project reflection by changing the verbs to past tense. In a sense, the 4Cs of Creative Expeditions provides a rubric for enabling inspiration to flourish and be assessed in project-based learning.

citizenship (bit.ly/2TWeAsb) through video creation.

3. What critical **content** is required?

   Identify the crucial elements that, when brought together, will create the optimal video to best visibly express the ideals of the project.

   GUIDING QUESTION: How well do these elements connect to successful criteria?

   INSPIRATION: Follow these eighth-grade documentarians through their process of curating content (bit.ly/2Uu5Q12).

4. What **constraints** bind this project?

   Identify constraints that are a part of this project. Evaluate the available materials, resources, and time.

   GUIDING QUESTION: How will I leverage constraints to create the best video project possible?

   INSPIRATION: See the incredible reflections that emerge when students are time-constrained to synthesize their learning in a thirty-second vlog (bit.ly/2K7SumX) after every robotics lesson.

14 WORLD WILDLIFE FUND PROJECT

Students will be inspired to research the issue of elephant poaching in Africa.

Grade Levels:
5–12

Time:
Three instructional days

Learning Goals:
Students will think with complexity and apply knowledge and skills to solve environmental and social issues. Students will conduct short research projects to answer a question, drawing on several sources and generating additional related, focused questions for further research and investigation.

Support:
During this project, students will storyboard, edit, find and create content, narrate, revise, and share their videos for assessment or peer review. Ensure students have clear goals for each of the actions and support them and provide direct instruction as needed.

INSTRUCTIONS

Students will research the impact of African elephant poaching on local communities, the international ivory trade ban, and the history of ivory and its uses. Students propose solutions to prevent poaching.

Encourage students to use Skype, Facetime, Google Hangouts, or similar platforms to chat with other students in Botswana, Tanzania, Zimbabwe, Kenya, Zambia, and South Africa.

In this hypothetical scenario, they are working with the World Wildlife Fund to create a documentary video based on their research and conversations with students in African countries. The video will contain clips taken by students locally and in the communities that are impacted by elephant poaching. To raise awareness, they will include cinematic elements and post their videos to YouTube.

Tips & Extensions

In addition to or in lieu of the solution video, students could create a public service announcement to raise awareness about wildlife crime and how to speak up for animals that have no voice. World Wildlife Fund (WWF) is an excellent resource that provides materials at worldwildlife.org that you can use to teach students about animals and wildlife conservation.

Asking your PLN on Twitter is a great way to find global classrooms willing to connect with you. Additionally, use a site that exists for this purpose like empatico.org.

SAVE THE ECOSYSTEM STEM PROJECT

Students will engage in a STEM project to find solutions to a local environmental problem (e.g., the decline in the salmon population in the local bay).

Grade Levels:
2–8

Time:
30 minutes

Learning Goals:
Students will propose solutions to the problem (e.g., return the salmon population back to its previous levels and therefore mitigate the environmental impacts of the declining salmon population). They will create a video to inform others of their solutions.

Support:
Encourage students to generate and compare multiple possible solutions to this problem. Some students may choose the first solution and run with that, but it's important that they evaluate all solutions and choose those with the biggest impact.

INSTRUCTIONS

1. Students will begin by researching the problem (e.g., the importance of salmon in the local bay [in this scenario, it's the Columbia Bay in Washington state]).
2. Students can look at related solutions (e.g., in addition to dam removal, other environmental changes impact salmon that can be reversed if action is taken soon, such as climate change, shoreline development and diking, dredging estuary marshes, and low-impact gardening and landscaping).
3. Students will create a video with their solution, download, and share it with school, community, and environmental groups via YouTube or email.

Tips & Extensions

Encourage students to learn more about their problem and what they need by supporting and tracking the work of local environmental groups. Encourage students to write letters and even share the videos they create with representatives to tell them they care about the problem, (e.g., salmon, steelhead, and orca populations).

16. IMAGINATION INQUIRY

Inquiry-based experiences are meant to encourage students to ask better questions to think more critically about a concept.

Grade Levels:	Time:	Learning Goals:	Support:
1–12	Two instructional days	Students will generate questions to think with higher complexity about a topic.	Teachers can use this tool to harness student imagination and curiosity. The imagination inquiry tool can help students ask better questions to guide them in the creation process while solving a cognitively complex problem.

INSTRUCTIONS

1. **LAUNCH:** Begin by sharing an interesting fact, problem, or dilemma with your students, and then guide them through the following protocol. At the end of the protocol, the students will have created a video with a response and supporting props and digital media.

   - Your teacher has shared some information with you that is intriguing. You already have some initial questions. What are they?

2. **IMAGINE:** Have the students review the questions they wrote. Each student should choose the question they find most intriguing, then build on that question by letting their curiosity run wild. Use the prompts that follow to tap into their natural inquisitiveness:

   - Create a metaphor that represents your question.
   - Share your metaphor with a classmate and ask him or her to build on your metaphor.
   - Suppose this concept played out in a different time or place. What would change?
   - What was the preconcept, pre-story, or backstory of this concept?

3. **CREATE:** Ask students: Choose the prompt that is most intriguing to you and articulate your thinking (through storytelling) by creating a narrative video.

4. **REFLECT:** Ask students: How did your thinking change from the first time you were introduced to the concept to after you created your product?

Tips & Extensions

When you ask students to create, give them a topic and then set them loose. Some students will start by researching on Google, and others might plan out what they'll create or discuss their ideas with friends. We want students to be excited to jump into this experience, but we also want to ensure they have all the support they need to engage in complex thinking throughout the process. Use this strategy before the creation phase in a project.

FRAYER MODEL

A Frayer Model is a great tool to help students activate prior knowledge while creating new learning. The strategy below is a new take on the Frayer Model.

Grade Levels: K–12	Learning Goals:	Support:
	Student will activate prior knowledge and build new learning by engaging in a video representation of a Frayer Model.	Teachers have the option of asking students to engage with the traditional Frayer Model (shown below in Figure 17.1) before creating a video representation.
Time: 1 hour		

INSTRUCTIONS

In a traditional Frayer Model, students write the word they are going to define in the middle of a graphic organizer. In the upper left corner, students write the definition of the word in their own words. In the upper right corner, have students write the facts or characteristics they know about the word. In the lower left corner, students write or draw an example of the word. In the lower right corner, students write or draw a nonexample of the word.

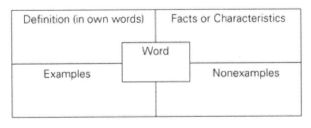

Figure 17.1

In the new video creation version, give students the freedom to represent the Frayer Model in the way of their choosing. Students create videos to represent the word, using media or real props of their choosing. Don't forget to remind them of the green screen features.

Tips & Extensions

This strategy is a lot of fun, and students get very creative. They will deepen their knowledge without feeling like they are "doing" school. This strategy is most effective if you assess students on their creativity and the depth provided in each aspect of the definition (e.g., examples, nonexamples [words or concepts that are the opposite or ineffective examples]).

EXPRESSING DILEMMA

This strategy supports students in elaborating on information by allowing them to describe dilemmas and challenges they experience while solving real-world problems.

Grade Levels:
5–12

Time:
Two instructional days

Learning Goals:
Students will engage in a structured academic discourse of a real-world dilemma.

Support:
This strategy is effective at the introduction of a project, unit, or essential question. It helps students think more expansively about a mathematics concept or a dilemma they are facing and enables them to find the support and mindset to push through challenges.

INSTRUCTIONS

I adapted the Expressing Dilemma Protocol from the Consultancy Protocol developed by Dunne, Evans, and Thompson-Grove to help teachers solve dilemmas in the profession. The eight steps of the adapted protocol help students solve dilemmas in mathematics, deepening and enhancing their understanding of content and material as well as supporting critical thinking and elaboration.

1. The teacher begins by organizing students into small groups of four to seven. One student is a presenter while the others act as the consultancy group that provides feedback.

2. The presenter gives an overview of the dilemma with which she or he is struggling and frames a question for the consultancy group to consider. The group's conversation should focus on the dilemma the student presenter faces. The consultancy group asks *clarifying questions* (i.e., questions that have brief, factual answers).

3. The group members then ask *probing questions* of the presenter. Probing questions help the presenter clarify and expand their thinking about the dilemma. The goal is for the presenter to learn more about the question she or he framed and to do some analysis. The presenter responds to the group's questions, although sometimes a probing question might ask the presenter to see the dilemma in a novel way, and the presenter might not have an immediate response beyond, "I never thought to approach the problem this way." The student group does not discuss the presenter's responses. At the end of ten minutes, the group leader or teacher asks the presenter to restate the question for the group.

4. The teacher frames a focus question for the student consultancy group. The question should address the dilemma at the crux of the problem. The focus question will guide the student group in its discussion of the dilemma. All students then critique the focus question. Questions they may ask include, "Is this question important to my dilemma?" "Is this question important to my learning?" or "Is this question important to others in my group?"

Fourth- to Sixth-Grade Example: You are part of the design team for a theme park. The residents of your town want a rollercoaster, a Ferris wheel, and a waterslide. The 0.5 × 0.5 mile area will traditionally allow for only two of these rides. How will you use this area to make the residents of the town happy?

Seventh- to Eighth-Grade Example: You are the CEO for a tech start-up that has developed an app to help tutor students in mathematics. The initial investment was $50,000. The software will cost $20,000 in engineering costs plus the amount of labor costs for software developers. How much more money will you need to operate the business in the first year? When will you be able to pay your investors? What will your cash flow be like? How much will you sell the app for?

Ninth- to Twelfth-Grade Example: The school wants to install a "green" roof. The roof is circular, and some room must be left for maintenance. What's the best way to create the maximum space for greenery and allow a small space for maintenance? Give dimensions and the shape of the space the greenery will occupy.

5. After sharing the dilemma with the small group, the presenter ends the description by asking a specific and thoughtful question, such as, "What do you really want to know? What is your real dilemma?" The dilemma is the problem group members face when tackling the question. Some things are known, so that information shouldn't be in the question (i.e., information specifically given in the scenario). This question will help the student group focus its feedback. "Yes" or "no" questions generally provide less feedback, so they should be avoided. With this step, presenters have the opportunity to tap into the thoughts of the group.

6. The group members then discuss the dilemma together. In this step, the group works to define the issues more thoroughly and objectively. Sometimes members of the group suggest actions the presenter might consider taking. If they do, they should frame them as

suggestions made only after the group has thoroughly analyzed the dilemma. The small group will create a video addressing the dilemma creatively.

7. The following question prompts will help guide students on what to address in their videos. Encourage students to be creative in the use of media, artistic style, music, etc.

Questions to Frame the Discussion

- Overall, what did we hear?
- What didn't we hear that might be relevant?
- What assumptions seem to be operating?
- What questions does the dilemma raise for us?
- What do we think about the dilemma?
- What might we do or try if faced with a similar dilemma?
- What have we done in similar situations?

8. After the group members create the video, they will share it with the student presenter. The student presenter then reflects on what they heard and what they are now thinking, then shares anything that particularly resonated during any part of the group work. This step should take about five minutes.

9. The teacher then leads a brief conversation about the group's observation of the consultancy process. This step should take about five minutes.

Tips & Extensions

The process involves a lot of steps and is meant to inspire in-depth conversations, not to burden students with an arduous process. Give students appropriate freedom within the protocol.

19 DIGITAL STORYTELLING AND ACTIVE LISTENING

Educators today encourage students to share their voices, spread their ideas, and develop communication skills through effective storytelling. However, to fully support student voices, teachers also must also develop the right conditions in which student voices can make an impact.

Grade Levels:
K–12

Time:
45 minutes

Learning Goals:
Students will share their thinking and express their understanding on an intellectual level, as well as reveal in detail how they think and feel about a particular experience or concept.

Support:
This project tasks the students with expressing a particular life experience. Before creating a video, it's important for the storyteller to consider the variety of ways their story may be perceived. Teachers can support this early process by having students first share their stories verbally while others actively listen. Doing this simple exercise provides real-time feedback to the storytellers. The storytellers can keep that feedback in mind as they move forward in creating their videos.

INSTRUCTIONS

Educators can employ four simple steps to encourage active listening and build empathy among students:

1. Listen to the student's story.
2. Paraphrase the story the student just shared.
3. Receive confirmation from the student that the story has been perceived the way they intended.
4. Allow the storyteller to reflect on the listeners' perspectives.

Here is an example activity that follows these steps:

1. Ask students to pair up.
2. The storyteller has three to five minutes to share their story. Here are some story starters:

- Because this happened this week at school, I want to change this next week.
- My teacher or fellow students pushed my thinking in this way.
- I tried something risky and it worked.
- I think I have this quality/characteristic because of this personal experience.

3. Listeners are silent until time is up.
4. The teacher will announce that time is up.
5. Listeners summarize the storyteller's message by restating the big idea and reflecting on the feelings they experienced when hearing the story.

- "So, I heard you saying . . ."
- "This is what I understand to be your emotion about . . ."

6. The storyteller gives feedback about how it felt to have the listener actively listen.

- "I felt like I had something important to share when you gave cues that you were listening to me."
- "I felt valued when you were focused on listening to my story."

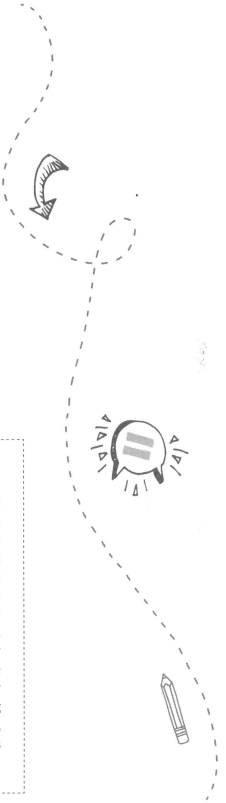

Tips & Extensions

This protocol for active listening can be applied to stories told in person and to stories told through multimedia such as video. The beauty of this framework is that it requires something from everyone involved. The audience is tasked with active listening and building empathy. At the same time, it's also important for the storyteller to actively take in feedback as they become aware of their audience. This multifaceted communication drives deeper collaboration and understanding among everyone involved. Active listening allows both the storyteller and the listener to develop a depth of understanding and provides a window into the storyteller's values, levels of thinking, emotions, and presuppositions behind their experiences.

FILM FESTIVAL

Let your students feel like film producers and movie stars!

Grade Levels:	Time:	Learning Goals:	Support:
K–12	Three instructional days	Students will build creative capacity through the production of a film.	Encourage students to think outside the box and use metaphors and similes. There are many English Language Arts (ELA) connections!

INSTRUCTIONS

1. Festival Theme: Films must respond to the theme of the festival. Themes can be centered around a unit of study, upcoming holiday, or upcoming community event. Students are invited to interpret the theme as they see fit, so long as audience members can clearly understand how the theme is used in the film. Encourage students to be creative with the theme. Push them to think beyond their first impressions and create a focus for a truly original film.

2. Successful videos are those that show clever stories from interesting angles. Therefore, teachers should encourage students to view videos that have won other film festivals.

3. Provide students with the following rules (from the Global Student Voice Film Festival [GSVFF]) studentvoice.org/#filmfest

4. Please review all of the rules carefully and comply with each. If any of the rules have not been followed, in fairness to others, that film will not be judged as part of the film festival. (Almost half of all submissions last year were

rejected for having ignored one or more rules.)

5. Films should be uploaded to any YouTube account with the "Public" privacy option.

6. The film should address the theme.

7. The film must be the original work of the student(s) submitting the video. (See below for the use of media content taken from online.)

8. The portion of the film addressing the theme must be no longer than 60 seconds, but you may use up to another 30 seconds for credits. The credits section cannot have any film content extending the story; anything after the one-minute mark should focus solely on giving credit to media citations and those involved in making the video.

9. One goal of the festival is to help students better understand digital citizenship issues related to intellectual property. Therefore, anyone entering will need to follow the very specific rules related to sources and citations (see below). Any image or audio used in the film must be "copyright friendly." For festival purposes, this means all images and audio used

must be made by the student(s), or Creative Commons–licensed content taken from specified websites (see the list of approved sites below). All video footage must be recorded by the student.

10. All media used must be properly cited in credits at the end, and we have provided models for you. See below for more specific instructions for each type of media and a model format for citations.

11. Because these films will be freely available online, you will need release forms for anyone identifiable appearing in the video. Release forms are not to be sent to the GSVFF unless requested; students should give these to the teacher, who will confirm in the online entry form that he or she has signed release forms for anyone identifiable appearing in the video. The committee will ask for scanned versions of all release forms for videos that make the finalist round. You may use release forms Next Vista for Learning makes available if your school does not already have something similar that parents approve related to content posted online.

12. Films must be appropriate for viewing by the general public, including elementary students (as with a movie rating of "G").

13. One may enter as many films as one wishes, but each one will require a separate entry form. We encourage the student(s) and teacher/adult sponsor to sit down together and carefully complete the entry form.

14. Films eligible for the finalist round will be scored using the scoring guidelines below.

15. Films must be in English or include English subtitles.

16. Sources and Citations: The credits should be a list of all the sources of the images and audio used in the film. Remember that for the GSVFF, all film footage must be recorded by the student(s) submitting the film. For this contest, students' material must be their own work or copyright-friendly content (i.e., media other than footage) taken from one of the following websites:

- **MUSIC:** AudionautiX.com, ccMixter, Incompetech, or the YouTube Audio Library.
- Students also may use the music offered in their editing software, as long as there are no restrictions running counter to the rules of the GSVFF. If students are using music from a video editor, they must include that in the credits as in the model below.
- **SOUND EFFECTS:** Freesound.org
- **IMAGES:** Wikimedia Commons, Pixabay, Unsplash, Openclipart, or Flickr
- Note that images must be Creative Commons licensed. For Flickr, link to search.creativecommons.org and choose the tab for Flickr, because this simplifies getting Creative Commons–licensed search results.
- Remember that any footage (film recordings) students use must have been recorded by them. Footage taken from an online source will disqualify the entry.

17. Citation Models: The closing credits should be a list of all the image and audio sources. These sample citations should help students decide how to plan their credits, an essential part of any successful film.

MUSIC: List the name of the piece, the artist, and the site from which it was downloaded. If the piece was created or recorded by the student, he or she must also provide a citation listing the software used to create it. Follow these examples:

- Corporation Motivation by Jason Shaw from Audionautix.com
- My Angst by Your Name created in GarageBand
- Happy Jingle from the WeVideo Music Library

SOUND EFFECTS: List the name of the effect, artist, and site from which it was downloaded. If the effect was created or recorded by the student, he or she also must provide a citation listing the software used to create it. Follow these examples:

- Crowd laugh.wav by Adam_N from Freesound.org
- Students Laughing by Your Name created using Soundtrap

IMAGES: List the name of the image, the name of the person who uploaded it, and the site. Note that the reason for going through the Creative Commons page is to ensure that students use copyright-friendly material. If the image was taken or created by the student, he or she must also provide a citation listing the date it was created. Follow these examples:

- Lamanai, Belize by joiseyshowaa from Flickr.com
- Fantasy-landscape-elephant-man-sun-2995326 by kellepics from Pixabay.com
- My Baby Brother Throwing a Tantrum by Your Name taken September 2018

This playlist of short videos can help you better understand Creative Commons as it relates to this festival: bit.ly/2GtBQua

18. Scoring:

    Power of the Story (15 points or 75 percent): Does the film convey a story that is compelling and addresses the theme? This represents 75 percent of the overall score, and students should be encouraged to spend plenty of time crafting their scripts and getting feedback from others.

    Technical Aspects (3 points or 15 percent): The focus here is on meeting basic concerns (appropriate lighting, spoken audio that can be easily understood, balanced volume, etc.). Although exceptionally well-produced films do have a small advantage, the key issues are the clarity, creativity, and compelling nature of the story.

Titles and Citations (2 points or 10 percent): Does the film include the use of titles and citations and make it clear for the viewer who is responsible for what was used? Note that if it is unclear that something has been cited (such as music that isn't explained in the credits), the film will not be judged.

Tips & Extensions

The film festival can occur in conjunction with a project-based learning project or it can be extracurricular/independent. The film festival should promote high levels of thinking and learning, and it should be integrated into the regular subject-area curriculum.

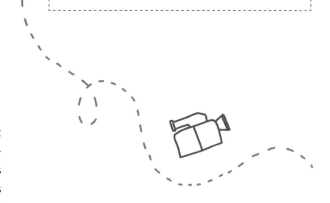

INQUIRY CIRCLES

Creating thoughtful questions for inquiry supports students in becoming more engaged mathematics learners.

Grade Levels:	Learning Goals:	Support:
3–12	Students will build critical thinking and metacognition skills through storytelling, inquiry, and reflection. This protocol empowers students to take control of their own learning through storytelling, inquiry, and reflection.	Betty Bisplinghoff developed the inquiry circles protocol to assist teachers in developing a deeper sense of inquiry. Teachers can use the protocol to generate questions about a mathematics project or challenge, with the goal of exploring how students think about mathematics, their frustrations, any challenges they are facing, and successes they've experienced along the way. The protocol has students sharing their mathematics stories, which supports and affirms their progress. Additionally, and especially with mathematics, students often feel as though they are the only ones who are experiencing frustrations.
Time: Three instructional days		

INSTRUCTIONS

This process facilitates a student-to-student connection that starts to give new meaning to learning together. Teachers can best use the protocol as a reflection exercise, although they also can use it to transition to a new concept that connects to a closely related, previously learned concept.

Phase 1: Storytelling (Day 1)

1. Give students time to reflect on their learning in their video journal (created via WeVideo). It may be helpful to advise students to begin by listing recollections about good things in their work and then choose one item on that list to explore in more detail through their video. The following prompts can nudge this kind of thinking:

- Think about times in this project when you felt like you were successful. Talk about and show those successful moments.
- Select one of those moments and create a video about this successful experience.

2. When students complete their reflective videos, they move to fill an empty seat in the "circle of inquiry." The "circle of inquiry" is made up of two groupings of chairs. A smaller circle is set up inside the other, with the two circles of chairs facing each other. Partner pairs are the students sitting knee-to-knee (one in the outer circle and one in the inner circle).

3. Students initiate the collaborative inquiry process by sharing their videos. These can be uploaded to a Google Drive or YouTube channel.

Partners will take turns sharing their video stories (thirty minutes total; fifteen minutes for each partner). Identifying words and phrases that emerge during the storytelling, as well as key concepts, themes, and ideas, can prove to be most helpful to each storyteller and listener.

- The storyteller shares his or her video.
- The listener records notes, capturing important features of the story being shared.
- The partner pairs then switch roles.

4. Each student reviews the notes he or she took during the partner's story. This is preparation for retelling the partner's story in phase 2 of the protocol.

Phase 2: Retelling Approximately (Day 2)

1. Reconfigure the inside and outside circle pairings into two sets of partner pairs (i.e., pair up everyone in the inside circle and also in the outside circle).
2. Follow and then repeat each of the following steps for every person in the group.

- The partner (the one who listened to the story in the previous phase) introduces the storyteller to the new group and retells the story that he or she heard.
- The storyteller has time to add to or clarify what their partner has shared. The storyteller uses this time to confirm the highlights their partner shared and add any other necessary details.

3. The group members ask clarifying questions. It is helpful to keep these questions focused on eliciting more information about what was "good" about the original story. This is not a time to make suggestions.

Phase 3: Crafting and Claiming a Positive Inquiry Question (Day 3)

This phase uses flexible timing. The group of four should agree on the amount of time necessary for individual reflection and whole-group dialogue.

1. Partners complete a video "storytelling recap" for one another based on the storytelling process and the questions that emerged from the group discussion. Once the partners complete their video recap, they share it with the storyteller.

- Each person reviews their notes from the storytelling experience and records responses on the recap sheet (a Google Doc). The recap is helpful in creating a shared set of data from the storytelling process and provides written documentation for the storyteller to use as a resource in crafting positive inquiry questions.

2. Partners give storytellers their recap sheet (or share via Google Docs). Students pause and personally reflect on what has been shared as well as what is recorded on the recap sheet. Students should use this time to consider how their personal experiences can serve as a starting point from which to craft an inquiry question that builds on some aspect of their reasoning and thinking that is good and strong.
3. Students craft a question for themselves and write it in the center of a sheet of chart paper or online in a collaborative document. For example:

- What really matters when solving problems?
- What do you want to carry with you in your problem-solving toolkit?
- What do you want to change?

4. Students move among the whole class group from chart to chart and silently participate in a written conversation around each proposed question. This activity provides an opportunity

for students to discuss the proposed questions, exploring and expanding the possibilities of the inquiry. The intent is not to answer or propose ways to resolve questions, but rather to explore related assumptions and ideas. At the conclusion of the debrief, each person has time to revise their question. The step ends with a go-round in which each student simply states their question for beginning an inquiry. It is understood that this question may go through several revisions once the inquiry is in process.

For a group rather than individual inquiry, during this step, the teacher reconvenes everyone in one whole group inquiry circle. Each person writes the themes their partner identified from their story on chart paper for the group to see. The teacher encourages the group to review the posted themes and discuss using the following prompts:

- Are there any additional themes or core values that need to be posted?
- Are any of these themes or core values related?
- Are any more important than others?
- Are any less important than others?
- Will any have greater or lesser impact on our work together?
- How can we carry forward what we value most?
- How can powerful work of the past inspire and support present needs to inquire?

Source: Adapted from Bisplinghoff, 2017.

Inquiry Circle Recap Sheet

1. What were the most compelling features of the story?
2. What was the most quotable quote that came out of this storytelling?
3. What was the most significant moment in the storytelling for you as a listener?
4. Did a particularly intriguing, innovative idea emerge during the telling of this story? If so, describe what you learned about it.

5. What three themes or core values stood out for you (how the other student expressed their thoughts, used a strategy you haven't thought of, and so on) in the story you heard?
6. What possible inquiry questions did you hear in the story?
7. Use positive language as you attempt to craft possible inquiry questions in support of your partner's work.

Tips & Extensions

This strategy builds critical thinking and metacognition skills. It also helps students understand the high value teachers place on learning and sets the tone for classroom expectations, especially for reluctant learners. Finally, it helps build listening and questioning skills for younger students early on.

REVISION PROTOCOL

22

When a student responds incorrectly to a question or does not articulate their thinking, the teacher should support students to strive for accuracy.

Grade Levels:
K–12

Time:
20 minutes

Learning Goals:
Students will strengthen their work through the revision process.

Support:
When students go back and revise work based on teacher feedback (via video), they will think about how they originally approached the concept or solved the problem and how they will now reason through a problem or approach a concept based on new feedback.

INSTRUCTIONS

The teacher provides video feedback, using a four-quadrant template as a guide. Fill out the quadrant sheet (digital versions like Google Docs or Sheets work well) with key points and then record a screencast, talking through the typed-out notes to provide students more detail. The top left quadrant is for strengths, the top right is for areas to review and revise, the bottom left is for recommendations, and the bottom right is for resources that might be useful to the student. It's important that the teacher provides feedback not only on the accuracy and precision of the solution, but on the thinking evidenced or not evidenced in the work. Additionally, recommendations can be written as questions to prompt students or support them if they're stuck.

Note: This is not meant to give students the steps or the "right answer," as this defeats the whole revision process.

Strengths:	Areas to review and revise:
Recommendations:	Resources:

Tips & Extensions

This is more of a teacher instructional strategy than a student activity. Students would rather receive an engaging video with feedback (and supporting visuals) than a standard document. Make the feedback process fun!

23 MORNING MEETING

Begin each day or class period by establishing a strong sense of camaraderie and community in the classroom, which ensures that students will be the most successful in their learning space.

Grade Levels:
K–12

Time:
20 minutes

Learning Goals:
Students will contribute to a positive learning environment by creating video messages that allow them to express their individuality.

Support:
Responsive Classroom (responsiveclassroom.org) suggests setting aside twenty to thirty minutes each morning for a morning meeting. For middle and high schools, a homeroom can be structured for every student to have a morning meeting together for twenty to thirty minutes. According to the Responsive Classroom morning meeting format, teachers and students interact purposefully using the following four components:

- **Greeting:** Students and teachers greet one another by name.
- **Sharing:** Students share information about important events in their lives. The listening students are encouraged to offer empathetic responses or ask clarifying questions.
- **Group activity:** Everyone participates in a brief, lively activity that fosters group cohesion and helps students practice social and academic skills (e.g., songs, poetry).
- **Morning message:** Students read and interact with a short, inspiring message written by their teacher. The message is crafted to help students focus on the upcoming work and learning that they'll be doing.

INSTRUCTIONS

1. Routinely ask students to discuss issues that matter to them and how they would create solutions.
2. Ask students to create videos about their differing worldviews, personalities, and backgrounds and how they have similar or different preferences. Students learn from one another why other concepts and problem-solving approaches are interesting to their peers.
3. Alternatively, ask students to identify their own personal hobbies, interests, strengths, and weaknesses in general. Then ask students to use visual representations via video creation to quantify these characteristics (e.g.,

"Create a video to show your strength levels in a particular subject").

Tips & Extensions

Morning meeting activities support a growth mindset for tackling or reviewing the previous day's concepts. Morning meeting is a great place to make real-world connections to mathematics, encourage students to explain their thinking, practice respectful conversations and debates, and remind students why they are solving problems.

RULES AND PROCEDURES

The shift from a teacher-centered classroom to a student-centered classroom does not mean the role of the teacher has diminished; actually, the opposite is true. The role of the teacher in the classroom has never been so important. The most successful learning occurs when the teacher is a facilitator or activator of learning.

Grade Levels:
K–12

Time:
15 minutes

Learning Goals:
Students will establish classroom procedures and norms by engaging with a teacher-created inspirational video.

Support:
Another important aspect of establishing rules and procedures is to provide a structure and frequency for communication and feedback with students and parents. In the past, teachers would communicate through grades, report cards, or phone calls to parents. But direct, everyday feedback to students will provide more specific and helpful feedback and will lead to greater learning growth.

INSTRUCTIONS

1. From the start of the school year or when students first enroll in class, teachers should clarify students' expectations for the class (i.e., ask the students what they'd like to get from class). This practice challenges conventional methods of instruction, in which the teacher tells the students what to expect. It begins the process of students co-creating learning goals and addresses any anxiety or misconceptions that students have about the teacher, class, or subject.

2. A great way to establish positive expectations is the creation of a fun "Behind the scenes" or "Hello from the future" video. In the video, the teacher might showcase the creative process, the willingness to figure things out, the courage to take risks, and the ability to laugh and learn from mistakes.

Tips & Extensions

Instead of simply giving students sets of problems or passages to read, teachers are designing learning experiences that build on student strengths. This in turn empowers students to create new connections and pursue more complex thinking by engaging with subject matter through real-life problem solving and perseverance.

Because of this instructional and professional shift, it's important that the teacher establish and communicate clear rules and procedures for students to set the stage for positive interactions and relationships between teacher and student and among students.

The most successful teacher–student relationships are built on safety, trust, and respect, and are those in which the student fully understands and shares the teacher's vision for learning success.

FRIENDLY DEBATE

Through this process, students can discover their voices, gaining both confidence and momentum to learn and spread ideas. Students can use video creation to exercise their creative processes as they respond to and reflect on issues that matter to them.

Grade Levels: K–12 **Time:** 45 minutes	**Learning Goals:** Students will engage in productive discourse while building creativity and communication skills.	**Support:** Exposure to fun and interesting projects leads to student-created videos and creates a solid foundation in the subject. More importantly, such projects can be designed to include options for students to investigate and discuss controversial concepts. Students will think on deeper levels when given the chance to debate possible solutions and discuss why an idea might be particularly baffling to them.

INSTRUCTIONS

The following protocol will help guide students in positioning themselves to conduct an effective debate:

1. Assign students to small groups of four to five students.
2. Within their groups, each student should present a response to a problem or scenario. After each presenter speaks, each student will offer responses to the question prompts below. Each student should share with the group their response to each prompt before all move on to the next. The prompts below were adapted from The 4A's protocol which considers assumptions arguments, agreements, and aspirations.

   - What **assumptions** does the presenter hold?
   - What do you **agree** with in their **argument**?
   - What do you want to **disagree** with in their **argument**?
   - What parts of the **argument** do you **aspire** to act on?

3. At the conclusion of the protocol, students will have their thoughts organized in a way that lends itself to use as a storyboard, the ideal starting point for an effective story for a student to communicate via video. The students would then create their video defending their viewpoint and argument addressing the conclusions from the protocol.

Tips & Extensions

To further leverage the creative processes of video creation, students can respond directly to each of the prompts through a brief video. Students could then decide which of those responses they want to include in their finished video product. Student-created video responses offer additional benefits in that teachers have evidence of student thinking and can therefore provide formative assessment feedback on how students applied the 4A's to the scenario.

Source: NSRF Harmony 4A Protocol

26 HISTORICAL DOCUMENTARY

Instead of writing a paper detailing a historical event, invite students to create a compelling story using real people and places in the past.

Grade Levels:	Time:	Learning Goals:	Support:
3–12	Three instructional days	Students will engage in history in a fun and engaging way through the creation of a historical documentary video.	During the project, find natural times during the learning block to meet with small groups to reteach any social studies or ELA concepts.

INSTRUCTIONS

1. Historical documentaries can be a part of the regular social studies curriculum or a part of a schoolwide history day. It's also helpful to choose a theme with which students can mount their ideas (e.g., courageous leaders, minorities in politics, the greatest acts of peace, etc.).

2. Before students begin their research, coordinate subject matter experts to visit the classroom (either virtually or face to face) to talk about their experiences surrounding the chosen theme.

3. After students have collected their data via scholarly articles, interviews, documentaries, and speeches, students develop their storyboards and scripts. Students should now have their plans for video production.

4. Students should use the WeVideo Essentials media library, which contains royalty-free audio, video, and images that are licensed and available for student use.

5. After the video has been layered and sequenced, finishing touches should be applied, and the videos should be shared via Google Drive, Facebook, YouTube, or another online platform.

Tips & Extensions

If students are recording voice-overs, encourage them to record in chunks so they don't have to re-record large sections when editing and revising.

BOOK REPORT

Try this fun, innovative twist on the traditional book report.

Grade Levels:	Time:	Learning Goals:	Support:
K–12	45 minutes	Students will provide their perspectives and reflections on a piece of text.	Small group instruction can occur simultaneously to address English/language arts standards (main idea, summarizing, characterization, author's purpose, fun, etc.).

INSTRUCTIONS

1. In traditional book reports, students would include the following:

   - The type of book report they are writing
   - The title of the book
   - The author of the book
   - The author's purpose for writing
   - The time when the story takes place
   - The location where the story takes place
   - The names and a description of each of the characters discussed
   - Many quotations and examples from the book to support their opinions
   - Major themes identified

2. These components can be transformed into an engaging "book trailer" by inspiring students to create a video providing their perspective on the key points.

3. Ask students to make an outline, script, or storyboard of the elements. Within the WeVideo platform, students may begin with the "Book Reports" template. This template is prebuilt with tracks of tips and preset layers for video, audio, green screen, etc.

Tips & Extensions

Teachers can also have students submit a writing piece along with the video, such as the script or student summary. It's important to give students feedback on the clarity of the submission and the level of expressiveness displayed. Feedback provided to students should address their progress around summarizing, comparing and contrasting, making predictions and connections, and considering different perspectives.

28. CREATION NAVIGATION

Students naturally crave ways to express themselves creatively, so how can we help foster that natural curiosity? This WeVideo strategy encourages, supports, and promotes the process of creativity.

Grade Levels:

K–12

Time:

Varies depending on student pace

Learning Goals:

Students will demonstrate creativity at higher levels by progressing through the four stages of the creative process and then documenting how they progressed through the stages.

Support:

Touch base with students throughout each stage. Help students that stay in the preparation phase use their passion and interests to guide them to the next phase, without pressuring them to move hastily.

INSTRUCTIONS

Cognitive Psychologist Scott Barry Kaufman at the University of Pennsylvania uses his neuroscience of creativity research to conclude that the creative process can be divided into four stages: **preparation, incubation, illumination and verification**.

Set aside time during the school day for students to progress through the creative process at their own rate. Below are some guiding questions and prompts students can use to help them successfully navigate the creative learning stages.

Guiding prompts for the 4 stages of creative learning

Preparation stage: At this stage, the brain is seeking information.

- What concepts am I studying at school right now that are the most interesting to me?

- What do I love to work on the most?
- I wish . . .
- I hope . . .
- This makes me really angry . . .
- This makes me sad . . .
- This makes me happy . . .

Incubation stage: At this stage, the mind simply wanders with no expectations.

- Go outside and wander. Let your thoughts take you wherever you want.
- There no expectations. Just let your curious mind wander.

Illumination stage: At this stage, connections between ideas are made. This is where we typically find the "a-ha!" moments.

- Did you notice anything new or interesting?

- Why was it interesting to you?
- How did it make you feel?
- Does it make you want to do something or solve a problem?
- How did what you noticed connect to something you're hopeful about or passionate about?

Verification stage: At this stage, creative ideas are communicated in a way that reaches an audience, articulating a purposefully constructed message about the student's creation.

- What does your creation mean to you?
- What does your creation mean to others?
- What visuals, music, etc. can best articulate your creation?
- How can you tell a compelling story about how your idea became a new creation, so that others can experience the process through their lens?

After students have answered the questions about their creation, they will then create a video about their creation and share it with each other or their community. The video should, in some way, demonstrate how they progressed through the creative stages, how their thinking changed throughout, new questions that emerged, challenges they encountered, and any new "a-ha!" moments.

29 MATH EXPLAINER

Inspired by Jennifer Eggert, instructional coach, Bloomingdale, Illinois

Students think at a higher cognitive level about math concepts when they show others how they solved a problem.

Grade Levels:	**Learning Goals:**	**Support:**
K–12	Students will explain and justify their thinking of a math concept.	Make sure students know that writing on a digital whiteboard does not need to be perfect. It's difficult to do, so it's all the more important that they explore and practice. Involve choice. Do all kids have to screencast? Can some create, some critique, and some engage in alternative forms of activity/assessment? Can it be an option on a choice menu? Make it collaborative. Pairing or grouping students allows for other super-awesome skills to emerge and be put to use.
Time: One instructional day		

INSTRUCTIONS

Introduction

- What is a screencast?
- *Audio* (Voice) + *Screen* + *You* (Student) (See "How to Create Screencast")
- Why do we screencast?

For the Student:

- Explain your mathematical thinking
- Think like a mathematician
- Sometimes it's easiest to explain in words
- Switch it up

For the Teacher:

- Way to see your understanding
- Provide help—do what's best for you

I Do: Model Screencasting Process from Start to Finish

Screencasting Process:

- WeVideo Academy Screen Recording Tutorial Video (wevideo.com/academy#axdxnoq5b5)
- WeVideo Screenshot Step by Step Directions Slidedeck (bit.ly/2UQGA6d)

1. Open up any other sites to be used for the screencast in different tabs (digital whiteboard, virtual manipulatives, etc. [see below for links]).
2. Go to *WeVideo, log in, Create New Video Edit, Title Video.*
3. Choose *Media,* then click on Red *Record* button.
4. Choose *Record Screen* option (you may be prompted to install the WeVideo Recorder Extension).
5. Start recording. Switch tabs to whiteboard or manipulative page.
6. Make the screencast. It should be less than three minutes.

- Introduce yourself by name.
- State your purpose, skill, or standard.
- Talk through each step: explain in detail everything moved, written, clicked on, etc.
- Use math vocabulary
- Incorporate thinking stems:
  - "I know this because . . ."
  - "Now I'm going to . . ."
  - "It's important to . . ."
  - Close with a "thank you!"

7. Click on the *WeVideo* Flag Icon. Choose *Stop Sharing*, save video. Once loaded, drag into the timeline from the media bank.

8. Listen to make sure the recording worked. Click *Finish*. Choose quality and saving location. Publish your video!

The following screenshots show the steps of this process.

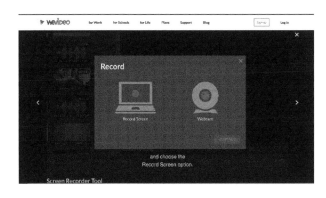

We Do: Evaluate a Student Example

1. Play student example (see the bank of samples at bit.ly/2vb7NAW)
2. PAUSE the screencast every time any positive or negative action is taken
3. Ask students to identify what they've noticed:

   - Volume, pacing, clarity, screencast time
   - Math language/vocabulary
   - Introduction, conclusion
   - Evidence of math understanding

4. Together, create a checklist or rubric with the class based on the discussion (see samples above)

Independent Work Prep

- Give students a sample task/problem.
- Allow students time to practice whispering to themselves and going through the steps of the recording process.
- Provide the focus task/problem for students (consider differentiating or letting students choose based on the standard/skill) either on

paper, projected, or digitally on each student's device.

- Example Display (bit.ly/2VO2Utr) note the different colored numbers for various students based on readiness level
- Project Screencast Criteria/Guide (bit.ly/2KO6zGH)

You Do: Student Screencasting

- Screencasting Process WeVideo Academy Screen Recording Tutorial Video (bit.ly/30ZZy9B), WeVideo Screenshot Step by Step Directions Slidedeck (bit.ly/2KXAjRE)

1. Open up any other sites to be used for the screencast in different tabs (digital whiteboard, virtual manipulatives, etc.; see below for links)
2. Go to WeVideo, log in, *Create New Video Edit*, *Title Video*
3. Click on red *Record* button, choose Webcam option (you may be prompted to install the WeVideo Recorder Extension)
4. Start recording, switch tabs to whiteboard or manipulative page
5. Make the screencast (less than 3 minutes)

   - Introduce yourself by name.
   - State your purpose/skill/standard, etc.
   - Talk through each step—explain in detail everything moved, written, clicked on, etc.
   - Use math vocabulary

   Incorporate thinking stems:

   - "I know this because . . ."
   - "Now I'm going to . . ."
   - "It's important to . . ."
   - Close with a "thank you!"

6. Click on the *WeVideo* Flag Icon. Choose *Stop Sharing*, save video. Once loaded, drag into the timeline from media bank.
7. Listen to make sure recording worked.
8. Click *Finish*. Choose quality and saving location. Publish your video!

Assessment/Now What?
- Gallery Walk: Students walk around and listen to each other's screencasts, giving feedback
- Suggested Elementary Peer Feedback Stems (bit.ly/2Usiyt4)
- Post on a blog (try Blogger), website (Google Sites), or global platform (you can even put student videos in a Google Slides deck or Doc and grab the shareable link to post on Twitter). Ask for feedback!

Tips & Extensions

- Use for peer teaching: Create a YouTube playlist of tutorials from your class, use it as a model with which to evaluate, and make it available for students who need extra assistance.

- Self-reflection: Use a written form or have a conversation with students so they can think metacognitively. Insert finished video into the student's digital portfolio (Sample Primary Template: bit.ly/2GkkVsS).

- Use their assessment to guide instruction and differentiation: What's next?

- Keep screencasts short. They should be no longer than four minutes.

- Allow students to whisper to themselves to practice beforehand. Let them conduct trial runs.

- Emphasize that you do not start over after starting a screencast. We're all human, and we all make mistakes. Instruct them to just say "oops" or "excuse me" and continue talking.

- Test recording settings before you begin.

- Start with an introduction and purpose statement. Close with a "thank you."

- Teachers will know who they're listening to, and students will understand their purpose and also practice manners.

- If students have questions during screencasting, let them know they must raise their hands to avoid disrupting the screencasting of others.

Provide kids with an "I'm Done" task to perform while they wait for others to finish, as they will all finish at different times. This task could be listening, reflecting on the day, and writing about how they'd like to extend their work.

LITERATURE CIRCLES

Small groups of students gather to discuss a piece of literature in depth.

Grade Levels: 6–12 Time: 45 minutes	Learning Goals: Students will form cooperative groups, read a short text, and engage in thoughtful discussions about literature through video creation.	Support: • Keep the text short but powerful and interesting to your students. • Don't require students to read aloud. • Ensure every student has a role and feels like they had a choice in the role.

INSTRUCTIONS

1. Prepare a Google Doc containing the following roles and descriptions:

   - **Facilitator**: Writes questions to guide thoughtful group discussion and keeps the group on task

   - **Director:** Writes out group members' connections to the text, including the director's, in preparation for the video

   - **Producer:** Writes a summary of the beginning, middle, and end, revises with group input, and creates the final book summary

   - **Word Wizard:** Searches for unusual word choice or description or defines words the group may not know

   - **"Inferer":** Selects and reads important passages or instances of descriptive imagery to the group and discusses the author's style

   - **Videographer:** Captures video of the reading and the debrief

2. Gather a stack of picture books or short texts for the practice literature circles.

Step 1: Introduce the unit with a short book talk about each book that a group may choose, or talk about what type of short text students will select. (See the Book Talk strategy in Strategy #4.)

Step 2: Explain the roles and group norms in literature circles. Allow students to choose groups or assign groups with three to six members per group.

Step 3: Each group chooses a text, and each group member chooses a role sheet for the practice round. Let students know they will choose different roles when they begin the novels.

Step 4: Circulate as students read the book or short text as a group. Do not force any student to read out loud, but most in each group will want to take a turn reading.

Step 5: As the book is being read, the videographer captures video. When the text

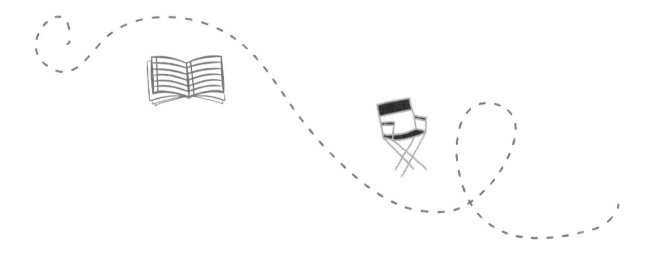

is finished, students will respond based on their group roles.

Step 6: The teacher circulates and offers suggestions for improvement as needed. The Producer and Director ensure the group discussion is rich enough to be included in the video.

Step 7: The students collaboratively create the video on the WeVideo platform, incorporating text images, audio, and any other props they feel would represent powerful imagery.

Step 8: As a class, "debrief" the Literature Circle experience. What do students think went well, and what could be improved?

Tips & Extensions

Create a proficiency scale or rubric for students in the group to self-assess their performances of their roles, comprehension of the book, and cooperative behaviors in the group.

31 ▶ BACK-TO-SCHOOL MESSAGE

An inspiring message that exemplifies those foundational aspects of the classroom can make for a strong classroom environment to survive the trials and triumphs of true discovery, failure, and learning that will take place over the year.

Grade Levels:

K–12

Learning Goals:
Students will convey a message using speech images, text, and sound regarding their thoughts about the beginning of school.

Support:
Reach students through video at the beginning of a new year. Video allows you to convey a message that can help build a deeper connection by including speech, images, text, and sound.

INSTRUCTIONS

Decide what you'd like your video message to be about. It could be anything, including setting expectations, classroom norms, building excitement for the learning that will happen, letting your students get to know you and one another, and setting up the scaffolding for a classroom environment that is truly fun, engaging, creative, supportive, and rigorous!

Here are four types of back-to-school videos you could make:

Idea 1: Setting Classroom Expectations

Setting up expectations and norms is important and makes for an effective and inclusive classroom experience. Try getting across your expectations in a fun way! Check out this video (bit.ly/2GsmVPA) from educators Tracy Stegall and Christina McCann, in which they send a message from the "future" to their sixth graders on how to take care of their computers. The bigger message was even more impactful:

the possibilities and dreams of what the students will be like in the future, and what their district's new 1:Web initiative aimed to achieve. You'll have a captive audience with something like this! Christina, the 1:Web coordinator, said, "I was surprised to hear the students spontaneously clap at the end of each video." Read more about their process here: bit.ly/2WPIAIq

What you'll need to make a Classroom Expectations video:

- Know the purpose of the message you want to share. Storyboard it!
- A green screen (use a green wall, a green sheet, or green butcher paper).
- Backgrounds (select several from the WeVideo Essentials Library, with over 400,000 images and video clips).
- Add other interesting graphics (the camera overlay in the video above and other effects are available in WeVideo Star Library).

Idea 2: Learning Goals

What better way to introduce learning goals than to do it in a way that piques a student's interest and curiosity? This book talk by Andy Jacks (youtube.com/watch?v=Go8szYsrmu4) got his students excited to read a book, especially when they saw two other wily students shrink him and steal away with him in a book.

What you'll need to make a Learning Goals video:

- Two student accomplices
- A green background and floor (Tip: use a long sheet of fabric or paper that drapes from wall to floor.)
- WeVideo's animation tool (to make teachers shrink)

Idea 3: A Glimpse into the Teacher's Life

Remember that feeling when you saw your teacher at the grocery store? It was kind of strange but exhilarating, right? Students are always curious about their teachers. Letting them in to know who you are, besides who you are as a teacher, can really help build those relationships. So why don't we let them have a peek into our worlds?

Here's one idea on how to make a video that taps into what students are already watching. "Routine videos" are SO popular on YouTube these days (bit.ly/2QABjKj). Routine videos are videos that show some sort of routine, like "My morning routine" or "My bedtime routine." You could create a video of your "Back to school routine."

One such video was posted to YouTube by @my2ndgradelife (bit.ly/2QBLi2j). This one aims at fellow teachers rather than students, so don't forget to remember your student audience when you storyboard your routine.

What you'll need to make a back-to-school routine video:

- Think about what your students would love to know about you.
- Film it!
- It's okay to leave out the parts you don't want to include.
- Add some text.
- Add music (you could pick from WeVideo Essentials Library, with over 100,000 pieces of music and sound effects).

Idea 4: Advice from the Previous Year's Class

This idea requires some backward planning, but this is a great idea from educator Christy Ireland of Buckingham Charter Magnet High School. She had her students create an "advice video" (bit.ly/2T-V5IJ3) for incoming students. What a wonderful way for students to reflect on how they have grown and to pass on that knowledge to the incoming class!

What You'll Need to Make an Advice Video from a Graduating Class:

- Ask students to reflect on the things that helped them be successful in your class.
- Provide a platform for them to jot down these ideas.
- Have students record, write, or take a picture of their piece of advice.
- Enlist some students to piece it all together.
- Add some fun transitions from WeVideo.

32 MAKERSPACE

A makerspace is a collaborative work space inside the school or classroom designed for making, learning, exploring, and sharing that uses high-tech and no-tech tools.

Grade Levels:	Learning Goals:	Support:
K–12	Students will explore and create meaningful video products based on ideas they've developed through projects.	WeVideo transforms the complexity of a TV studio into a stress-free learning experience. Video creation makerspaces can have permanent homes in libraries or small classrooms or can even be stored in bins/cabinets in a classroom. They also could have their own permanent spaces in the classroom.

INSTRUCTIONS

A makerspace doesn't always have to look like "shop class" or a robotics lab. In this case, it could be a video creation studio. Video creation makerspace studios might include green screen curtains or walls, recording devices (e.g., laptops, cell phones, tablets), and any props that students might want.

To set up a video creation makerspace, the following are nice to have:

- **Studio and Lighting:** The school will need a space to house the television studio and equipment. The room should be well-ventilated to cope with the heat of the studio lights and should include plenty of power sockets for all TV station equipment. Studio lights will give a more professional look to broadcasts, but modern video cameras operate well in natural or standard room lighting too.
- **Video:** High-definition video cameras (e.g., cell phones, tablets) mounted on tripods are good to have. Laptops also can be used.

- **Audio:** Handheld microphones or clip-on microphones are a must to ensure the presenters, interviewers, and interviewees can be heard properly. Camera operators will also need headphones linked to an intercom system to allow them to receive instructions from the producer or director.
- **Content Library:** The WeVideo Essentials Library contains many graphics, videos, and audio clips to embed.

Tips & Extensions

If the makerspace will also function as a school TV station, an audio mixer and a video switcher should be included. These two devices connect to form the hub of the school's TV station. Editing and mixing video and audio can all be done in the WeVideo platform.

DIARY/JOURNAL REFLECTION

Traditional written journal entry turned fun and creative.

Grade Levels:
K–12

Time:
15 minutes

Learning Goals:
Students will think critically about a learning experience and provide their reflections through the creation of a video diary.

Support:
Encourage students to show their personalities in the video diary. Provide sentence starters or diary prompts to increase the quality of reflections. (See Strategy #6, Exit Ticket.)

INSTRUCTIONS

1. Let students know in advance that after the learning experience, they will record a reflection via a video diary entry. Advanced notice allows them to metacognitively prepare.

2. After a presentation, math task, Socratic seminar, or group discussion, allow students to find spaces in which to record their entries. This can be done at their desks or at your video creation makerspace. If students need alone time, allow them to record at home or find a supervised place at school where they can spread out.

3. Provide students with ideas and prompts to guide their reflection:

   - How do you feel your presentation went?
   - Did you express your ideas during the group discussion?
   - How do you feel about getting peer feedback?
   - What would you do differently next time?

4. The actual recording should be no longer than five minutes, as this is meant to be a quick formative check during closure or at the end of a learning block.

5. Ask students to share their videos in their student folders on Google Drive.

Tips & Extensions

- Video diaries are most effective when used as closure or reflection of a specific learning protocol experience, discussion, or presentation, because students have a concrete experience to reflect on.

- Provide feedback on each video diary submission. Focus the feedback on the quality of the reflection.

- Provide feedback on the student video diary submission through a teacher-created video, and drop it in the respective student Google Drive folder.

34 ACADEMIC CONFERENCES

An effective way to connect and better understand students' learning progress, goals, and feelings about school.

| Grade Levels: K–8 Time: 10 minutes | Learning Goals: Students will use video to plan and set goals, reflect on their work, and reflect on the progress they've made in their learning. | Support: Typically, student–teacher conversations are held in real time. Creating a video provides an opportunity for students to share freely without the pressure of a face-to-face conversation. Even though prompts are provided for students, be prepared to meet with students face-to-face if they have difficulty responding to prompts. |

INSTRUCTIONS

1. Create a list of objectives that you want to address with each student. These can be topics that you want to discuss, strategies that you want students to learn and use, or even behaviors that you want to address. These objectives will be differentiated and individualized. Encourage students to include any questions and concerns in their video academic conference.

2. Questions and prompts for students:

- How do you feel about this class? School?
- What is something you did this week that you're proud of?
- What was an obstacle you overcame in your learning journey?
- What can you do to improve next time?

3. Respond to student videos with a teacher-recorded video. Affirm their reflections.

4. Any concerns you need to address or questions you have should be addressed face-to-face.

Tips & Extensions

- Plan this activity for a time when the other students are busy working in stations or small groups. Students can go one at a time to a "recording tent" or quiet place to record their videos.

- Video conferences are a great way to keep track of how students are progressing in class. Make sure you mix in conferences with face-to-face conversations.

WORD STUDY

As an alternative to spelling tests, this allows students to learn word patterns rather than memorize unconnected words.

Grade Levels:
K–8

Time:
20 minutes

Learning Goals:
Students will investigate and understand the patterns in words.

Support:
Knowledge of word patterns means that students don't need to learn to spell one word at a time. It is also designed to build word knowledge that can be applied to both reading and spelling. Creating a video word study helps build meaning out of words because of the use of imagery.

INSTRUCTIONS

1. Provide a spelling inventory to determine students' various stages of spelling development. Select a group of words that demonstrate a particular spelling pattern and sequence these patterns to match students' development.

2. Provide a list of words for students to sort. (This can be either hard copy or digital.) When sorting, students use their word knowledge to separate examples that go together from those that don't.

3. Students may look for words in their reading and writing that fit the pattern being studied. When these words are identified, ask students to create a video illustrating examples of the different patterns identified. Encourage students to use imagery to represent words and use the titles tool to place words in their video.

4. Take, for example, the difference between "hard c" (as in *cake*) and "soft c" (as in *citrus*). After collecting many words containing the letter *c*, students discover that *c* is usually hard when followed by consonants (as in *chalk* and *crawfish*) and the vowels *a*, *o*, and *u* (as in *cap*, *cost*, and *cutlery*). In contrast, *c* is usually soft when followed by *i*, *e*, and *y* (as in *circus*, *celery*, and *cycle*).

Tips & Extensions

- Ask students to identify their own words they would like to add to the list, using the patterns they have identified.

- The video created can be used as a formative assessment in lieu of the traditional spelling test.

36 PHOTO STORY

Instead of asking students to write a paper or report, ask them to create a photo story.

Grade Levels:
K–12

Time:
1 hour

Learning Goals:
Students will explain and reason through a new concept by creating a photo story.

Support:

This is a great alternative to asking students to research a topic and write a paper or to read a story and do a book or lab report.

Provide guidance on how their imagery connects to their topic:

- How will you represent fractions visually?
- Can you find current-day images to portray past histori-cal events?
- What kind of music was popular in the time period you are researching?
- What were your favorite parts of the story, and how will you represent them?
- What were your observations from the science investiga-tion and how will you include them in your video?

INSTRUCTIONS

1. **Prepare assets:** Ask students to gather the photos and graphics they will use in their pho-to story and upload them to WeVideo. They can upload them straight from their comput-ers or devices, or if they have them stored in a cloud service website, connect to it from WeV-ideo and pick them from there.

2. **Assemble the story:** Students will select the clips they'd like to use and drag and drop the images onto the Storyboard. If they use the multi-select feature, they can set the duration (in seconds) for the photos and imitate the Ken Burns style. They can always manually add photos by dragging them onto the Storyboard.

Each photo will be five seconds long by default. Remind students that they are not only assem-bling images in a sequential way but they are also telling a story to match the sequence.

3. **Polish:** To give their story a professional look, they can choose one of the WeVideo themes. Themes include music, transitions, title cards, and lower thirds that will look great with your photos. By default, the "Simple Theme" is selected, but they can change that at any time. Once the theme is applied, have students open each clip and add some captions. Captions will display differently depending on the theme selected. Some come with an animation and,

for them to display correctly, students must set the clip duration to a particular time (approximately seven seconds). They should preview the video to see the progress or choose another theme to see whether it fits better with their story. Students also can replace the song or adjust the volume.

4. **Publish and share:** All videos are automatically published to WeVideo. From there students can share a link or even publish to social channels (i.e., Google Drive or YouTube).

 **JIGSAW**

Members of a group become "experts" in a particular area and share their learning/research with the other group members.

Grade Levels:
6–12

Time:
Two instructional days

Learning Goals:
Students will explain a new concept by working in expert groups and creating a video as their presentation.

Support:
Provide students with prompts that align to the content standard (i.e., What are the organs and their functions that make up the body system you chose? What would happen to this body system if another organ in another body system failed?).

INSTRUCTIONS

1. Each member of a small group takes on a portion or aspect of a topic or skill. For example, if the subject is the human body, each student in the group is assigned a body system. More than one member of the team will take on the same portion/aspect if there are more group members than portions/aspects.
2. The team splits up, and everyone goes to an "expert" group of all the students from all the teams taking on the same topic (e.g., all the circulatory system experts will get together). The "expert" group masters the topic/skill or conducts the necessary research.
3. The "expert" group will create a video of their learning, using content from the WeVideo Essentials. The expert groups share their videos within a YouTube channel (e.g., Body Systems).
4. Synthesis is done in the teams as they watch the videos together.

Tips & Extensions

Encourage students to be creative with their expert videos. For example, a student may use Claymation or stop-motion (see Strategy #39) to show how the circulatory system works.

NEWSLETTER

A more engaging and student-centered take on the standard classroom newsletter.

Grade Levels:
K–12

Time:
Two instructional days

Learning Goals:
Students will use creativity and literacy skills to create a classroom newsletter.

Support:
Many times, teachers create newsletters to be sent home or shared with parents of students. This is an opportunity for students to use communication and collaboration skills to articulate classroom happenings and student learning.

INSTRUCTIONS

1. Decide on a grouping format. Will each group of students create a newsletter, or will each group be responsible for a section of the video newsletter?

2. In their groups, students will select the topics they'd like to discuss (e.g., current and upcoming projects, recent video field trips, makerspace reflections, etc.).

3. Brand your newsletter or section of the newsletter. Students will create a logo or tagline that can be used to brand every newsletter (e.g., Writing Corner, Math Geniuses, etc.).

4. Students will outline and create a sequence for their newsletter or section.

5. Encourage students to roleplay, wear costumes, and interview other students or community members. Encourage students to choose engaging text, images, audio samples, and other video elements.

6. Students will share their video newsletter in a teacher-designated location. The teacher will provide feedback and allow students to revise before sharing it on public social channels.

Tips & Extensions

This is a great assessment activity because it allows students to reflect on their learning. It also promotes student ownership as they "brag" about themselves and the work they have been a part of.

STOP-MOTION AND CLAYMATION

Stop-motion is a video art form that allows students to manipulate physical objects to create an animation. Traditionally, clay was used for the objects in the animations, but anything can be used!

Grade Levels:
K–12

Time:
Varies depending on the project. (The video creation process should take approximately 30 minutes.)

Learning Goals:
Students will explain their thinking of a concept through the creation of a stop-motion video.

Support:
This is a great strategy for teaching time and measurement.

INSTRUCTIONS

In this example, students create a stop-motion video on photosynthesis.

1. Students take still photos of a bean plant growing in the window over the course of days and weeks.
2. If the object doesn't move on its own, students will take pictures of objects and will manually move them to create the effect of movement when all the images are eventually sequenced.
3. Inside the WeVideo platform, create a new video or choose the "stop-motion" template.
4. The stop-motion template has preset tracks for text, audio, video, stop-motion (a series of still images), and voice-over (so students can narrate what's happening).
5. When students add photos, they may change the duration of the photos to create their desired effect.

Tips & Extensions

Select all photos at the same time to be dropped in the stop-motion track timeline.

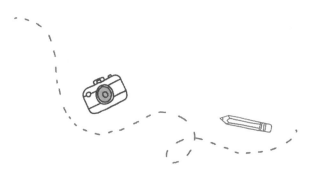

PUBLIC SERVICE ANNOUNCEMENTS

Let students promote their message through a public service announcement (PSA) video.

Grade Levels:
K–12

Time:
Three instructional days

Learning Goals:
Students will develop their communication skills through storytelling with music and timing elements to create the right mood and impact.

Support:
Support students in structuring the elements of a PSA (i.e., setting, issue, tone, feelings, problem, solution, and reflection) into a video while simultaneously encouraging them to insert their own designs. Ensure they include the following elements:

- A relevant issue to research and cover
- Five to ten cited facts to support their stance on the issue
- PSA video template for video creation optional)

INSTRUCTIONS

1. First, identify and research an issue of their choice. Example topics include world hunger, cyberbullying, texting and driving, mental health awareness, gender identity, or an issue of their choice.

2. Students will cover a significant issue that impacts their lives in a one-minute PSA video.

3. This project is powerful because it empowers students to take a well-informed stance on today's issues and provides a platform for discussing a complex topic in a supported format. The one-minute format requires students to be purposeful in their message, understand their audience, and be able to back their claims in a concise and impactful way.

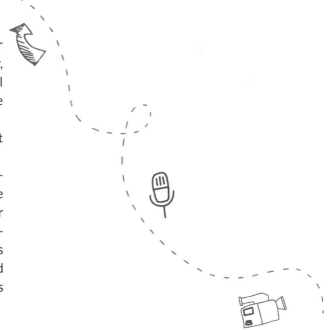

CONCLUSION

Students are more than a score. The video creation process naturally supports ongoing discovery, reflection, and growth. I believe in supporting students in their learning and growth from beginning to end. Rather than passively consuming media, I believe in actively creating it, providing tools for students to communicate in effective and compelling ways through video. WeVideo is on a mission to empower students to discover their voices to make an impact in the world. To fully support student voice, conditions must exist in which their voice is heard and recognized. Students should be engaged in learning that is both meaningful to them and mirrors the world outside the classroom. With WeVideo, students see how their work impacts their lives and the lives of those around them. True creativity is fostered by balancing open exploration and expression of ideas with support and guidance.

BIBLIOGRAPHY

"Appendix A: The Framework for Teaching." usny.nysed.gov/rttt/teachers-leaders/practicerubrics/Docs/Teachscape_Rubric.pdf.

Bisplinghoff, Betty. "Inquiry Circles: A Protocol for Professional Inquiry." schoolreforminitiative.org/download/inquiry-circles-a-protocol-for-professional-inquiry/.

WeVideo, "BTS 2018-2019." bit.ly/2TV5IJ3.

Dunne, Faith, Paula Evans, and Gene Thompson-Grove. "Consultancy." *School Reform Initiative.* schoolreforminitiative.org/download/consultancy/.

National School Reform Faculty (NSRF Harmony). "NSRF Protocols and Activities… from A to Z." nsrfharmony.org/protocols/.

"Responsive Classroom." responsiveclassroom.org.

Tsay, Emily. "Creating a fun video from "The Future" to share expectations with 6th grade students." WeVideo. bit.ly/2WPIAIq.

The HyperDoc Handbook

Digital Lesson Design Using Google Apps

BY LISA HIGHFILL, KELLY HILTON, AND SARAH LANDIS

The HyperDoc Handbook is a practical reference guide for all K–12 educators who want to transform their teaching into blended-learning environments. *The HyperDoc Handbook* is a bestselling book that strikes the perfect balance between pedagogy and how-to tips while also providing ready-to-use lesson plans to get you started with HyperDocs right away.

The Space

A Guide for Educators

BY REBECCA LOUISE HARE AND ROBERT DILLON

The Space supports the conversation around revolution happening in education today concerning the reshaping of school spaces. This book goes well beyond the ideas for learning-space design that focuses on Pinterest-perfect classrooms and instead discusses real and practical ways to design learning spaces that support and drive learning.

Innovate with iPad

Lessons to Transform Learning

BY KAREN LIRENMAN AND KRISTEN WIDEEN

Written by two primary teachers, this book provides a complete selection of clearly explained, engaging, open-ended lessons to change the way you use iPad with students at home or in the classroom. It features downloadable task cards, student-created examples, and extension ideas to use with your students. Whether you have access to one iPad for your entire class or one for each student, these lessons will help you transform learning in your classroom.

Classroom Management in the Digital Age

Effective Practices for Technology-Rich Learning Spaces

BY PATRICK GREEN AND HEATHER DOWD

Classroom Management in the Digital Age helps guide and support teachers through the new landscape of device-rich classrooms. It provides practical strategies to novice and expert educators alike who want to maximize learning and minimize distraction. Learn how to keep up with the times while limiting time wasters and senseless screen-staring time.

The Google Apps Guidebook
Lessons, Activities, and Projects Created by Students for Teachers

BY KERN KELLEY AND THE TECH SHERPAS

The Google Apps Guidebook is filled with great ideas for the classroom from the voice of the students themselves. Each chapter introduces an engaging project that teaches students (and teachers) how to use one of Google's powerful tools. Projects are differentiated for a variety of age ranges and can be adapted for most content areas.

Code in Every Class
How All Educators Can Teach Programming

BY KEVIN BROOKHOUSER AND RIA MEGNIN

In *Code in Every Class*, Kevin Brookhouser and Ria Megnin explain why computer science is critical to your students' future success. With lesson ideas and step-by-step instruction, they show you how to take tech education into your own hands and open a world of opportunities to your students. And here's the best news: You don't have to be a computer genius to teach the basics of coding.

Making Your School Something Special
Enhance Learning, Build Confidence, and Foster Success at Every Level

BY RUSHTON HURLEY

In *Making Your School Something Special*, educator and international speaker Rushton Hurley explores the mindsets, activities, and technology that make for great learning. You'll learn how to create strong learning activities and make your school a place where students and teachers alike want to be—because it's where they feel energized, inspired and special.

Making Your Teaching Something Special
50 Simple Ways to Become a Better Teacher

BY RUSHTON HURLEY

In the second book in his series, Rushton Hurley highlights key areas of teaching that play a part in shaping your success as an educator. Whether you are finding your way as a brand new teacher or are a seasoned teacher who is looking for some powerful ideas, this book offers inspiration and practical advice to help you make this year your best yet.

The Google Cardboard Book
Explore, Engage, and Educate with Virtual Reality

AN EDTECHTEAM COLLABORATION

In *The Google Cardboard Book*, EdTechTeam trainers and leaders offer step-by-step instructions on how to use virtual reality technology in your classroom—no matter what subject you teach. You'll learn what tools you need (and how affordable they can be), which apps to start with, and how to view, capture, and share 360° videos and images.

Transforming Libraries
A Toolkit for Innovators, Makers, and Seekers
BY RON STARKER

In the Digital Age, it's more important than ever for libraries to evolve into gathering points for collaboration, spaces for innovation, and places where authentic learning occurs. In *Transforming Libraries*, Ron Starker reveals ways to make libraries makerspaces, innovation centers, community commons, and learning design studios that engage multiple forms of intelligence.

Intention
Critical Creativity in the Classroom
BY AMY BURVALL AND DAN RYDER

Inspiring and exploring creativity opens pathways for students to use creative expression to demonstrate content knowledge, critical thinking, and the problem solving that will serve them best no matter what their futures may bring. Intention offers a collection of ideas, activities, and reasons for bringing creativity to every lesson.

The Conference Companion
Sketchnotes, Doodles, and Creative Play for Teaching and Learning
BY BECKY GREEN

Wherever you are learning, whatever your doodle comfort level, this jovial notebook is your buddy. Sketchnotes, doodles, and creative play await both you and your students. Part workshop, part journal, and part sketchbook, these simple and light-hearted scaffolds and lessons will transform your listening and learning experiences while providing creative inspiration for your classroom.

Bring the World to Your Classroom
Using Google Geo Tools
BY KELLY KERMODE AND KIM RANDALL

We live and work in a global society, but many students have only a very small community or neighborhood as their frame of reference. Expand their horizons and help them increase their understanding of how they fit in the global landscape using Google Geo Tools. This book is packed full of how-tos and sample projects to get you and your learners moving forward with mapping, exploring, and making connections to the world around you.

50 Ways to Use YouTube in the Classroom
BY PATRICK GREEN

Your students are already accessing YouTube, so why not meet them where they are as consumers of information? By using the tools they choose, you can maximize their understanding in ways that matter. *50 Ways to Use YouTube in the Classroom* is an accessible guide that will improve your teaching, your students' learning, and your classroom culture.

Illuminate
Technology Enhanced Learning
BY BETHANY PETTY

In *Illuminate*, author, educator, and technology trainer Bethany Petty explains how to use technology to improve your students' learning experiences. You'll learn specific how-tos for using a wide variety of apps and tools as well as the why behind using technology. Meet your students' needs and make learning memorable using technology enhanced learning.

The Martians in Your Classroom
STEM in Every Learning Space
BY RACHAEL MANN AND STEPHEN SANDFORD

In *The Martians in Your Classroom*, educator Rachael Mann and former Director of Space Technology Exploration at NASA Stephen Sandford reveal the urgent need for science, technology, engineering, and math (STEM) and career and technical education (CTE) in every learning space. Proposing an international endeavor to stimulate students' interest in science and technology, they highlight the important roles educators, business leaders, and politicians can play in advancing STEM in schools.

More Now
A Message from the Future for the Educators of Today
BY MARK WAGNER, PHD

The priorities and processes of education must change if we are going to prepare students for their future. In *More Now*, EdTechTeam Founder Mark Wagner, explores the six essential elements of effective school change: courageous leaders, empowered teachers, student agency, inspiring spaces, robust infrastructure, and engaged communities. You'll learn from educational leaders, teachers, and technologists how you can make each of these essential elements part of your school or district culture—starting now.

40 Ways to Inject Creativity into Your Classroom with Adobe Spark
BY BEN FORTA AND MONICA BURNS

Experienced educators Ben Forta and Monica Burns offer step-by-step guidance on how to incorporate this powerful tool into your classroom in ways that are meaningful and relevant. They present 40 fun and practical lesson plans suitable for a variety of ages and subjects as well as 15 graphic organizers to get you started. With the tips, suggestions, and encouragement in this book, you'll find everything you need to inject creativity into your classroom using Adobe Spark.

The Top 50 Chrome Extensions for the Classroom
BY CHRISTOPHER CRAFT, PHD

If you've ever wished there were a way to add more minutes to the day, Chrome Extensions just may be the answer. In *The Top 50 Chrome Extensions for the Classroom*, you'll learn time-saving tips and efficiency tricks that will help reduce the amount of time spent in lesson preparation and administrative tasks—so you can spend more time with students.

ABOUT THE AUTHOR

Nathan D. Lang-Raad, EdD, is a speaker, author, and professional learning facilitator. He is the chief education officer at WeVideo. Throughout his career, he has served as a teacher, assistant principal, university adjunct professor, consultant, and education strategist. He was director of elementary curriculum and instruction for Metropolitan Nashville Public Schools, as well as education supervisor at NASA's Johnson Space Center. He speaks at both local and national professional conferences and is the cofounder of Bammy Award–nominated #LeadUpChat, an educational leadership professional learning network (PLN) on Twitter. Nathan is also the cofounder of #divergED, a Twitter chat focused on divergent thinking and innovations in education. He is a Google Certified Educator, Microsoft Innovative Educator, and 2016 Apple Teacher, and he serves on the board of the Student Voice Foundation and the International Literacy Association Task Force.

Nathan is the author of *Everyday Instructional Coaching* and *The New Art and Science of Teaching Mathematics* (coauthored with Dr. Robert Marzano).

His work has been featured online by *EdTech K–12, Corwin Connect, Education Week, K–12 Blueprint,* and *Solution Tree.*

Nathan received a bachelor of arts degree in general science–chemistry from Harding University in Searcy, Arkansas; a master's of education degree in administration and supervision from the University of Houston-Victoria; and a doctorate of education degree in learning organizations and strategic change from David Lipscomb University in Nashville, Tennessee.

He resides with his husband, Herbie Raad, in Maine.

To learn more about Nathan's work, visit drlangraad.com or follow him on Twitter: @drlangraad.